Pages of Passion Book 4: Threads of Destiny

An Autobiography

George Hatcher

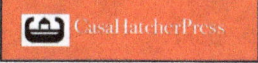

Previously published as Billion Dollar Rainmaker Part I in 2021

This book can be purchased at over 40,000 bookstores and libraries including brick and mortar stores, online, in print and digital, including Apple, Kindle, and Audible formats. Casa Hatcher Press is a subsidiary of Pretty Face, Inc. Rancho Mirage, California 92270.

Casa Hatcher Press. http://casahatcherpress.com (800) 416-6189

Copyright © 2025 by George Hatcher. All rights reserved. Printed in the United States of America and abroad.

No part of this book may be used in any manner except in the case of brief quotations in critical articles or reviews.

Book and cover designed by Casa Hatcher Press

Pages of Passion, by George J. Hatcher

First Edition June 2025

Library of Congress Control Number: 2025934438

ISBN: 979-8-9919018-5-7 (Hardcover)

ISBN: 979-8-9919018-9-5 (Paperback)

ISBN: 979-8-9919018-8-8 (eBook)

Author's Note

True Reflections: Echoes of a Life Remembered

As you embark on this journey through my life, I want to share a crucial aspect of my storytelling. While the names of individuals, places, and establishments may have been altered to protect their identities and privacy, and while memory may sometimes falter and details may blur with time, one truth remains unwavering – the essence of the story is real.

In this tapestry of recollections, woven with threads of honesty and nostalgia, what stands firm amidst the changes and uncertainties is the authenticity of my experiences. So, as you delve into these pages and navigate the twists and turns of my narrative, remember this: no matter the alterations, no matter the imperfections in remembrance, the heart of the tale beats with the rhythm of truth.

Introduction

Previously, on Pages of Passion... A Look Back Before New Beginnings

My journey has been anything but conventional. At seventeen, while serving in the U.S. Navy, I impulsively married Selena. This led to a reckless decision to go AWOL, fleeing to her hometown in Mexico where I attempted to build a new life by opening an ice cream parlor. However, the shadow of my past and the FBI's warning of impending arrest if I didn't turn myself in by my eighteenth birthday loomed large. The dream of that life shattered when, just days before that birthday, I discovered Selena's affair with her former fiancé, ending our marriage.

A desperate escape followed, with Selena's sister driving me across the border hidden in a car trunk. Though I intended to surrender to the Navy in San Diego, fear and

Introduction

hesitation led me instead to a grim Tijuana jail, from which I practically begged the shore patrol to return me to the USA.

The consequences were steep: a four-month sentence in a Marine brig. Upon release, instead of returning to my Navy term, I was immediately arrested by Los Angeles detectives for grand theft – an allegation stemming from borrowing $3,500 from a girlfriend's mother under false pretenses when I was about fifteen. This resulted in a sentence to the California Youth Authority, and I was sent to Deuel Vocational Institution (DVI), a place far harsher than any juvenile hall. In total, my incarcerations, including county jail awaiting trial, spanned about 27 months.

Paroled for a year, I quickly found work as a janitor in a downtown Los Angeles department store. There, I met Alicia and her roommate Clara, and together we became involved in a dubious activity known as the "locker thing". Opportunity soon knocked in the form of an apprenticeship in Air Conditioning and Heating, making me a union member with significantly better pay. My personal life, however, remained turbulent; after dating for over a year, Alicia became my second wife, a marriage that lasted only about 24 days.

Following this quick divorce, I moved from my parents' home to an apartment in Monterey Park, California. There, I befriended my new neighbors, Ava and Emma, who were call girls operating out of their apartment.

Introduction

It wasn't long before a new business prospect emerged: the chance to buy a body, fender, and paint shop in East Los Angeles. It was a sizable shop with great potential, but I lacked the capital. Despite this, I made the bold decision to quit my union job and purchase the business. My personal life saw another turn as I married Sophia, my third wife, who gave birth to our daughter, Judy.

The auto shop rapidly transformed into what I called the "cash cow," producing over ten car paint jobs a day, alongside bodywork. I expanded further, adding a mechanic department and a car upholstery department, and took on numerous collision jobs authorized by insurance companies. However, this success brought a significant challenge: I had to front all repair costs, often waiting weeks or even months for insurance payments. This created severe cash flow issues. To navigate this, I developed a system of cashing checks with check-cashing businesses, asking them to hold the checks until I had the funds to cover them, a practice that grew as I expanded to multiple shops. Las Vegas winnings sometimes helped bridge the gaps.

In these bustling early days of the main shop, I hired Elena to answer phones. She quickly learned the business, writing insurance estimates and preparing invoices, and eventually moved in with me. Her aunt and brother operated a mortuary business. As the business grew, I also hired Susie and Alexa to assist on the shop floor, and Mike, an acquaintance from my time in DVI, joined the

Introduction

team, working at the main shop and later at the new locations I opened.

This period of intense business building, financial maneuvering, and evolving relationships sets the stage for the "New Beginnings From Broken Dreams" that lie ahead...

Pictures In This Book

Dear Reader,

As you embark on this journey through my life, I want to share a unique aspect of this autobiography. Alongside my words, you will find a handful of selected images that complement my stories and memories. While these photos are not direct representations of the individuals I've written about, they serve to illustrate and evoke the essence of my experiences. For instance, a friend is referred to as Elena in this narrative, but it's important to note that "Elena" is not her real name, and the AI-generated image representing her does not depict her alone; it captures the essence of a character playing the part of Elena in my book.

In reflecting on my life, I've included images of significant people, places, and moments that shaped who I am today. From a stock photo of a child delivering canned food—reminiscent of my industrious youth when I sold canned goods I received from my father—to a vibrant portrayal of lettuce in the fields, reminding me of the days my dad took me to the lettuce fields, where workers picked lettuce and loaded his truck with crates of it, these visuals add another layer to my narrative.

Additionally, I've illustrated elements of my father's business, particularly a striking image of garlic, which represents the hard work and dedication that defined his life. These images are not just decorative; they are meant to enhance your understanding and connection to the stories I share.

Thank you for joining me on this personal journey. I hope these images enrich your reading experience and allow you to visualize my memories as vividly as I have.

WARNING!

Adult matter

This book is designed for an adult audience. It contains themes of violence and sexual behavior that are not suitable for minors, sensitive readers, or individuals living in the current chaotic world, where incurable sexually transmitted diseases and a pandemic have confined us to solitary spaces within our homes. While my life is not a work of fiction, the names of some individuals I have encountered have been altered to preserve their privacy.

All of the characters, organizations, and events depicted in this novel have likely been shaped by the passage of time, forgetfulness, and a timeline that was adjusted for the sake of expediency.

Also By George Hatcher

Mario 1: Woman in Jeopardy

Mario 2: Coming of Age

Mario 3: Risky Business

Mario 4: Free Fall

Mario 5: Afire

Mario 6: Marked

Mario 7: Aftershock

Mario 8: Captivated

Single Titles

One Wilshire

Gabi

Rico

Cats: Meow Is The Language Of Love

HER: Artistic Expressions Through AI

Elegance In White: Through Wedding Gowns

Quinceañera Fashion: Fifteen & Fabulous

Billion Dollar Rainmaker Part I

Pages of Passion Book 1: My First 19 Years

Pages of Passion Book 2: Bold Beginnings

Pages of Passion Book 3: Rising Waves

Beyond The Scale: Health Benefits of Keto for Wellness

Cool Under Pressure: Warm With Humor

Love Is What It Is: Lessons From Everyday Life

Living Fully While We Wait to Die: Mindfulness Amid Mortality

Coming Soon

Pages of Passion Book 5

Pages of Passion Book 6

Pages of Passion Book 7

Mario 9

Gabi 2

Rico 2

Dedication

Molly,

In the dance of life, you are my steady partner,

and in every melody, you are my cherished harmony.

With enduring love,

George

Chapter 1
A New Pad

The hills of El Sereno rise above a neighborhood that had seen better days – a bit blighted, run-down, though not quite squalor. Higher up in those hills, contractors were building new, appealing homes, though perhaps not as grand as those in Monterey Hills, where I currently lived. My eye, however, fell hard on two brand-new split-level houses going up side-by-side. Each boasted a lap pool, three bedrooms, three-and-a-half baths, monster living rooms, dens, dining rooms, and big kitchens. Views worth savoring stretched from most windows.

I was instantly smitten. One way or another, I was getting one of them, maybe both. I didn't phrase it quite that bluntly to Elena, my partner, who shared my life and, usually, my ambitions.

I showed Elena the house I slightly preferred of the near-identical pair. She agreed it was gorgeous and, a practical plus, much closer to the auto body shop we ran together.

The reason I was considering *both* houses involved Mike, my closest friend. Our bond had been forged years ago through the shared hardship of county jail and later, DVI. He and his girlfriend, Vicki, currently lived in a rental apartment on the West side, convenient only to the restaurant where Vicki waitressed. I showed Mike the houses, planting the seed for him to take the one next door to ours.

Elena, ever perceptive, didn't take long to ask, "Why are you involving Mike in the house next door?"

"I want to help him out," I said, perhaps a little defensively. "If he gets it, he has to pay, not me." Setting Mike up often felt like the right thing to do, even if it complicated things.

The contractor, Chuck, was already a customer of my auto painting business; we'd painted four of his smaller work trucks. The bigger ones were too large for our spray booth, and painting outside the booth was something I avoided unless it was a quick spot job on a repair.

Elena, Chuck, and I met in my office at the shop.

Chuck laid out the options: "I can sell them to you, lease with an option to buy, or just rent with sixty days' notice either way."

"What if I rent it and you decide to sell it later?" I asked.

"For now, renting suits me fine," Chuck replied. "I'm building nine homes up there. I'm in no rush to sell."

Elena, with her characteristic boldness, teased him. "Are you funding all this building you don't 'need' to sell with a little something extra, Chuck? Selling weed on the side?"

Chuck just winked at her, offering no denial, no confirmation, just that practiced look of innocence that always made us laugh.

"Tell you what," he offered. "If I do decide to sell while you're renting, I'll give you the right of first refusal."

"Meaning what?" I clarified.

"If I get a legitimate written offer from someone else, I bring it straight to you. You'll have the right to buy the house for exactly one dollar more than that offer. If you pass, then you'd have sixty days to vacate. Same deal if you're renting and decide to leave – just give me sixty days' notice."

Elena could have gone either way on the house itself. She'd previously mentioned being content in our Monterey Hills apartment, happy with her jogging routine and the complex's pool. I countered, painting a picture of jogging through these new, scenic hills and lounging nude in our *own* private lap pool whenever the mood struck. That argument seemed to gain traction.

I had a decision to make within two days – take one house, or commit to both.

Elena brought up her reservations again. "Baby, I like Mike, I really do, but do we need him living right next door? You know how he gets when he drinks. Please, baby. I just don't want him *that* close." Her concerns weren't unfounded, given Mike's history.

Mike, meanwhile, reported that Vicki was absolutely thrilled with the house, willing to commute across town to her restaurant job daily. He claimed her tips were good, which seemed plausible. The rent was set at three hundred dollars a month for each house, plus a five-hundred-dollar security deposit each. Through a furniture service, we could furnish each house completely for two hundred dollars a month on a one-year contract, or buy everything outright for two thousand dollars per house upfront. Their decorator would handle everything, including window treatments for the main rooms. (Two thousand dollars was a hefty chunk of change back then, especially for furniture.)

"Baby, you're digging into your Vegas stash for this," Elena pointed out, referencing the money I kept aside from my last Vegas win. "We don't *need* this."

"I'll walk away right now if you tell me you honestly don't like the house," I countered.

"I love the house," she admitted. "I already told you my objection is Mike living next door. The only other thing is you keep looking for places to spend your lucky dollars you won."

I decided to bite the bullet. I negotiated with Chuck to pay one year's rent upfront for *both* houses, and in return, he gave me a discount and waived both security deposits, saving me a thousand dollars right there. I also opted to pay the four thousand total to buy the furniture outright for both places. The decorator's service was a fantastic perk; they did a great job. The furniture wasn't high-end, but it looked great to me at the time and was exactly what we needed to move right in.

Then I told Elena a necessary lie: that I still had a binding lease on our old apartment and would have to keep paying rent there for a while.

"If you had told me *that* before," she said, her lips puckered in disapproval, "I would have suggested you pass on the house deal." She chose her words carefully – "suggested" – ever since a past argument where she'd accused me of hiding tax papers, she'd become more cautious in her phrasing during disagreements.

But I loved Elena just the way she was, even when she was annoyed with me.

Less than a month after signing all the paperwork and paying Chuck, we moved into our new house. The wide, three-car garage easily accommodated my car and Elena's Mustang. At one end, a fully equipped washroom stood ready with a washer, dryer, and ironing setup.

We walked through the spacious house together, marveling at the sheer size of it compared to our previous places.

Later that night, we stood in the darkened living room, looking out the big picture window. The view over El Sereno, stretching towards parts of downtown Los Angeles, was most stunning at night – the dark expanse punctuated by countless city lights. El Sereno itself was undeniably picturesque: houses climbing the hillsides like steps, palm trees silhouetted against the sky, red tile roofs glowing faintly, and more undeveloped land visible then than exists today. Cool blinds and drapes stood ready to shut it all out when we wanted privacy.

"It's been a while since I lived somewhere I could really stretch my legs like this," I mused.

"Not since the tiny apartment you shared with wife number three?" Elena asked, aware of my past marriages.

"Almost right," I clarified. Sophia is my third wife, my daughter Judy's mom. After that tiny apartment I rented a house about the size as this one but Sophia decided to leave and live with her grandmother who took care of my daughter while she was at work.

"Damn, you've been through a lot," Elena said softly, wrapping her arms around me.

"I love this," I said, pulling her closer. "One of the best parts is we didn't have to hassle with picking out furniture. And another best part? I know exactly where a chunk of the money from my last big win went."

"Oh baby," she sighed affectionately. "You give so much of your money away."

"I do not."

"You do too."

* * *

Mike had not expected I would front the money that I did to get his house. I was going to tell him he had to pay me back, but I didn't get around to it. We had gone through so much together at the county jail, then DVI. It was a real bond. He came over frequently, always with this distinctive knock before he came in.

* * *

Sunday morning Elena and I had breakfast and were heading back to the bedroom. At least I was. Elena came at me from the side, and I fell onto the couch with her on top of me. We ended up play-wrestling naked in the den on the sofa. She was on top of me. The wrestling morphed into necking and fooling around, with no sex. Mike did his knock. Or maybe he did or didn't. We didn't hear the knock or him walking in the front door, nor did we hear him wandering around the house until he found us in the den.

He was carrying a bottle of Canadian Club.

Six a.m., and he was wandering the house with a bottle of Canadian Club. What the fuck?

Elena screamed. It was not a frightened scream. It was a scream at Mike.

"What the fuck are you doing in here?"

She got disentangled from me and stormed at him bare ass naked. Mike was grinning like he did, but she started hitting him.

"Get the fuck out. And from now on, ring the fucking bell."

"I knocked," Mike said, holding up the bottle to block her blows.

I stayed where I was on the sofa in the den. I was laughing. That fucker. I heard the door shut, which told me Mike was out of the house. Elena was back and furious.

"Baby, it's not like we were doing anything."

"We're bare ass," she said. "We were close enough. And that doesn't matter. He didn't have any business walking in like that."

'He's seen your bare ass before," I pointed out.

Elena started punching my chest, but she wasn't serious about it. Eventually, we laughed it off.

"Fuck me," she said.

"Oh, Mike turned you on."

"Like we didn't just spend half an hour naked-wrestling and rubbing our bodies together? Think what you want; just do me."

I was so hard. How could I resist?

* * *

At first, I visited Mike's shop every day. Then I stopped going over. I talked to him on the phone and saw him often.

He was my neighbor. Vicki was always away at work. Mike would get home, and she'd be in later. Her absence gave Mike time to sit around, watch TV, and drink. If I wanted to drink with Mike, Elena's objections would not have stopped me, but the urge to drink was not there. Mike's visits to the house were short. I felt bad, so I'd go check on him when I knew he was waiting for Vicki to get home.

Mike never complained about my absence at his shop. I gave him some slack so I could see what he could do without my constant input.

When Mike went short thirteen thousand in his first month, he acted on his own. He went out and got the money, cashed checks, and rushed to make deposits to cover the checks he had outstanding. He banked with Kitty. I was on the account, but I made no inquiries of Kitty nor calls to check balances. I had my hands full with my other shops.

"I'm not being critical," Elena said. "I was thinking about how you went to all that trouble to rent from the Armenian, spent all the time and money to fix it up, and it was all for Mike."

"No way. I own the shop. He has all the headaches, and the deal is he gets a third of the net income."

Elena made a face. "I hope you are right."

"Hey, seems strange you seem to keep poking at Mike. You fucked him. Was he that bad that you're pissed at him?"

I didn't know why I said that. We were in the office eating, alone as always. She put the uneaten beef sandwich she was eating back in the box it came in, dabbed her mouth with a napkin, got up from the sofa, and went out the door. I remember sitting there suddenly not wanting to eat anymore. I looked out the window down to the shop floor and saw her talking to Susie. She walked out of the Brooklyn Avenue entry. Her purse was on the corner of my desk, right where she left it in the morning when we came in.

I came down from the office. Susie wasn't with a customer.

"Where did she go?" I asked.

"She walked up Rowan. I'd say to her aunts. She told me she wasn't coming back today."

"I pushed the wrong button," I said. "Do me a favor. Her purse is up in the office. It's on my desk. Run it over to her."

"Right away," she said.

We had driven in my car that morning. Elena's car was at the house.

When Susie got back, she was perspiring. "I didn't actually mean for you to run. Jogging would have been fine," I said with a laugh.

"It's okay. I ate bread for breakfast. I needed to burn it off, anyway."

"Did she say anything?"

"She said thanks."

Susie and I handled the afternoon customers and phone calls. I went to the house. I didn't stop for food. I was there for a while, not long, then went home number two. I didn't bother with food. I poured a CC water. Sat in front of the TV in the living room. I had three drinks alone. It was a record for me, drinking alone. Maybe I should have gone home, but I was home. Or I wasn't. Home was with Elena. The house was for Elena and me. From the start, I didn't believe she was truly hooked on it like I was. There was no point in being there without her.

When you're used to sleeping together, it's not so easy to fall asleep alone, but the alcohol helps. At nine or so, I fell asleep in my bed with the TV on. I don't know what time it was. I thought I heard a door, but thanks to the drink, I wasn't fully awake. I stirred when I felt breath against my face, maybe the movement of the bed as she got in, the comforter wafting over me.

I woke slowly.

I moved my hands just a little and touched a warm, naked body. Then she was kissing me. An instant later, I was participating in the kiss.

Elena was home.

"I'm sorry for being a bitch. If it means anything, the cramps are bad."

I kissed her and hugged her tight.

"How did you know where I was?"

"You weren't at the house. I figured you came over here to fuck Ava and Emma."

"You're bad," I said.

She kissed me with heat. "I love you, George Hatcher."

"I had three drinks," I confessed.

"I can smell it," she said.

I think that's when I dropped back to sleep.

* * *

In the morning, we smiled a lot, said a few words, and both of us slipped on our running shoes.

"If you hurt, don't jog," I said.

"It won't hurt me. I want to be with you."

I kept the pace down, but her pace was our regular pace. I stopped holding back.

"Last night, I took a taxi to the house. Then I drove over here in my car."

"I'm glad we slept together."

"I thought I'd find someone with you," she said.

"I had no takers," I kidded.

"Bull," she said. "You were just tired."

"Actually, I had three drinks. Hefty ones. Knocked me out."

"You confessed last night," she said. "How's the hangover?"

"None," I said. "Three drinks don't do me that bad."

We were almost at the foot of the steep hill.

"Tell me," she said. "I want to hear you say it."

I slowed the pace a little as I turned to look at her.

"I love you, Elena."

"Bitchin'," she said, looking straight ahead.

I don't think there was a single day when I didn't have to patch a money shortage. The good thing is that there were more small money shortages than big money shortages. In the third month, Mike gave me a check for two thousand dollars, sort of a dividend. It was supposedly my two-thirds dividend since he opened.

"That's what the Donald says I owe you," he said.

Mike was paying himself three hundred fifty dollars a week, a little more than I used to pay him, plus one-third of the net profit if there was a net profit. Plus, he had his fringe benefits: the bit I gave him when I came back a winner, plus a furnished house for him and Vicki for a year, rent-free.

When I showed her, Elena was totally surprised.

"I'm going to copy and frame it," she said.

"Don't be so mean."

"I'm not being mean. It's neat."

The following month, Mike got a new Impala.

"How did you swing it?"

"Small down payment and Kitty financed it."

It was the way he said it—the way he said her name, the way he said she financed it. I knew before I asked, but I had to ask.

"Totally cool, Mike. Let me guess, are you-"

"G, she's older, but she is a hot fuck."

Not that much older. I'm pretty sure she wasn't thirty yet. "You didn't."

"I did. She egged me on."

I laughed.

"You not pissed?"

"What would I have to be pissed about? -- Congratulations."

"Brother, thanks."

We shook hands. He had a stupid grin on his face.

"What about Vicki?" It was dumb for me to say that.

"What about her? I shower, and Kitty's evidence is gone." More grinning. More handshaking.

I told Elena about Mike and Kitty.

"That body of his," she said.

"If you like his body so much, why are you rude to him at the house?"

"He drinks too damn much. That's the biggest problem," she said.

I had the decorator leave one bedroom without furniture. I had planned to put together a gym in there. Jogging was keeping me trim, but it wasn't sculpting the parts that had Elena drooling. I wanted to believe that I didn't have a jealous bone in my body about anyone or anything.

* * *

After lunch, I caught Jose on his back doing sit-ups in a small corner behind the upholsterer's section.

"What's this?" I asked.

"I heard from the mechanic at Mike's that Mike had five of the team over there doing sit-ups and pushups after lunch. So, I was just testing it out." He made this huge burp. "Maybe I should have waited longer after lunch."

Elena heard this and laughed. I didn't laugh.

"Baby let it go," Elena said. "You better than anyone know how he is. Remember when he was here? He used to do pushups and sit-ups every chance he had. Right over there." She pointed to the spot next to the upholstery department where Jose had been.

I shrugged. "I'm not saying anything. You're right. It's the way he is."

Jose said, "I hear everyone loves working with Jefe Mike."

Before I could say anything, Elena said, "It's good for business."

I nodded in agreement.

I wondered if Elena had fucked him again or was planning to. Was I keeping score or what? It stings me because it's Mike. It stings me that she asked him to do it. Damn. It's been so long - why am I even thinking about it now?

The sale of insurance company receivables to Sam was handled on a monthly basis. Mike turned all claims he had over to Sam, and he'd get a check back payable to Whittier Auto Center for eighty-two percent of the total amount. The first month, Mike had only one finished insurance job, and he gave it to Sam because he needed the money. Now in his fourth month, it was more. Although it still pained me to forfeit the eighteen percent, I understood it was simply the cost of doing business, much like cashing checks that came with a daily fee.

In the past, having the receivables was always to blame for being short at the end of the month. With more shops and more employees, that changed. Even after I received the check from Sam, I came out short. [1]I had to run to Chester and or Rene to get cash against checks I would give them. I didn't keep tabs on Mike to save myself the worry, but I knew Mike dealt with the same problem, only with a smaller dollar amount than mine.

Mike was not good, only at blackjack. He was a dynamite poker player. I couldn't tell by his facial expressions how it was going at Whittier Auto Center. It's hard for me to believe I really wanted the distance from his shop, but there just wasn't room in my brain for more stress. The insurance companies were sending business there, but

---

1. To cover a temporary $5,000 business shortfall needed for creditors, I utilized a specific arrangement at a check-cashing establishment with the help of contacts there, Chester or Rene. I would write them a check for $5,000. Instead of depositing it immediately, they would give me the $5,000 in cash, which I then deposited into my business account to meet supplier payment obligations. Chester or Rene agreed to hold my check until I confirmed my account had sufficient funds to cover it. Once I notified them the funds were available, they would deposit the check. For this service of delaying the deposit, I paid them a fee calculated based on how many days the check was held.

without Sam buying the paper at the end of the month, the place would crash. His paint business was close to nothing. I seriously thought of doing another salvage restoration there to help make ends meet, but I didn't want to interfere. It's also not that easy to find the right salvaged car to restore.

Chapter 2
Too Much Booze

I enjoyed the new house so much that I needed a drink in my hand to savor it. The drink helped me get with the tunes that we always had playing on the hi-fi. I did not think I was drinking to escape the business headaches.

A couple of times a week, Elena brought food from the grocery store to cook. She had a thick cookbook and really got in it. She made pasta, watched me eat, and asked me over and over again if I liked it. She cooked a dynamite-loaded hamburger. She bought a heavy-duty fryer small enough to go on the kitchen counter, but it kept blowing fuses. There went the French fries. It was no great loss. We were happy.

On Sunday, when Vicki didn't work, we barbecued at Mike's house. Steaks on a grill don't take much skill. But Vicki fixed some great potato salad, macaroni salad, and macaroni and cheese. She was a fantastic cook. When we were over there, Mike out-drank me three to one.

I could tell that Elena got turned off seeing him drunk.

* * *

I drank almost every night. Elena made my drinks. That meant there was less liquor in them than I put in. I was okay with less liquor. I couldn't really tell. Elena might finish one drink to my three. I didn't need an excuse, but Elena often said it was the pressure of the shops, my insistence on maintaining excellent credit, and turning out work that customers totally loved. In my mind, I was too young to cave to such pressure. I just liked to drink and didn't need a reason. That's how you get when it becomes a habit. It's addictive that way, like gambling.

* * *

The living room had a nice tufted sofa with two matching chairs that faced each other with a small table between them, kind of like my stuffed chairs at the apartment, only these were much nicer. Cheap, but the look was expensive.

Elena and I were seated facing each other.

"Baby, I'm going to stay at my aunt's house for a while."

I put my drink on the table. "Why?"

"I'm making you drink after drink. I keep thinking you are on your way to being like[1] Ramirez. I can't do it."

---

1. Ramirez sold me my first shop, the cash cow, as I called it, on

"I don't think I've ever been drunk," I said. "Tell me if I have."

"You're right. You can drink. It used to be one drink. Now it's four or five. Last night, it was six. I don't want to do this."

"You're leaving me?"

"I'll continue to work with you."

"Is it just the drinking?"

"It's the drinking."

"I'll stop drinking."

She smiled when I said I'd stop drinking.

"When you do that, if you want me, I'll come back."

"Baby, if you leave, will you jog over where you're going?"

She laughed. "I don't think so. No one jogs over there. I think you're tipsy."

Maybe I was tipsy. I wasn't drunk. I was tired. I went to bed at the far end, my back to her. I felt her behind me. She kissed the back of my head, and when she kissed my shoulders, I went out.

In the morning, she didn't jog with me. She stayed back to pack.

I dreamed of her beautiful eyes. Her brows and lashes

Brooklyn & Rowan. Ramirez started drinking every day at five in the afternoon. He was a drunk.

were black and perfect. Elena's eyes were so beautiful I have trouble describing them. They were black like her hair.

Elena

The hills where the house was were aggressive mothers. I chopped along that day alone. I forced myself not to give up. It would have been easy to stop and head for home. I pushed myself. The more I ran, the more I smelled the liquor as I sweat, a nasty smell to remember. I wiped away what should have been sweat under my eyes, but I'd swear it was pure alcohol.

I got strong under the pressure.

Fuck it. I've been alone before. Fuck it.

I thought of making up with my wife, Sophia. Was that even possible?

I called her. She cut me off. She did that almost every time I called.

Let's see, wife one, down. Wife two, down. Wife three, on the way down. Girlfriend Elena, exiting stage left. Good thing I kept the apartment.

Fuck it.

When I got back, coffee was ready, but she wasn't in the kitchen. I got out of the shower, dressed, and got ready to leave.

"I'll be twenty minutes behind you," she said. "See you at the shop."

I didn't know what to think on my way to work. I wasn't sure if I was happy or heartbroken not to be tied down to one woman. But as the day went by, it became harder and harder for me to accept that Elena's clothes would no longer be in my closets.

She was so cool about it. Instead of lunching with me, she drove her car to her aunt to unload her suitcases at noon.

George Hatcher

Susie acted like she was unaware like she didn't know anything, but I knew she knew.

Chapter 3
Donna

After the morning rush, I called the host at the Flamingo, who said he'd fix me up with a suite and anything else I needed, all comped. I didn't have to pay; they gambled on the probability the house would beat me this time. Before I left work, I let Elena know where I was going. At two in the afternoon, I was on a plane to Las Vegas. I arrived with nothing, but the free suite had toiletries, and two men's shops were on the first floor. The suite was fabulous, clean, spacious, stocked, and especially free.

I went to the lobby but didn't go to a table. I sat on a stool at the bar where I had never before sat down for a drink. Donna, a brown-eyed blonde from Georgia, sat beside me. I didn't detect an accent, but what did I know about accents back then? For fifty, Donna would spend two hours with me. A hundred would buy all night. She was cute, a Marilyn Monroe look-alike with a fabulous smile, about my age. The hotel wouldn't let minors hang out at the bar where she found me. She was legal, for sure.

On the way to the penthouse elevators, we stopped at the 'we sell it all' shop. While Donna looked around for a bubble bath, I had the lady behind the counter get me a quart of Canadian Club.

"I've never been in this suite before," Donna said, walking around. "This is huge, you lucky man."

I opened the bottle of CC and asked her if she wanted a drink. "You have wine?"

Behind the bar were two refrigerators and an ice maker. One of the fridges boasted a wide assortment of wine. That night, when I was with Donna, I knew nothing about wine.

"White or Red?"

Pages of Passion Book 4: Threads of Destiny

Donna

* * *

"Red. Sweetie, are you doing the overnight? That way, no rush?"

I found a corkscrew and opened the red merlot.

"All night is good. Want money now?"

"Pay later. I know you won't screw me."

Not knowing any better, I handed her a full glass of wine.

"I plan to screw you, but not out of money," I said.

"That's funny," Donna said.

I poured my Canadian Club and could hear Elena in my head. "Baby, don't pour so much. Let me make it for you."

I clicked glasses with Donna. No question, she was pretty. That fair hair and blue eyes were a novelty to me.

"Sweetie, is it okay if I take a bubble bath in one of your bathrooms?"

"Of course, but just one thing. Call me G or George, not Sweetie."

"G is your name from now on."

I raised my glass to her.

I had no change of clothes. I was being a wacko. A dumb ass. Why was I here?

I knocked on the bathroom door and walked in, finding Donna under a blanket of bubbles.

Pages of Passion Book 4: Threads of Destiny

Donna

"I got to run to the mall to get a change of clothes," I said. "I'll be back. Make yourself at home."

"G, there's two stores in the lobby."

"I just need a regular store," I said. "I'll be back."

When I got in a taxi, it was seven at night. "I need to buy jeans, shirts, socks, and underwear."

"We have one mall, the Parkway Mall on Maryland

Parkway, a big line up one-story shops, and they close at nine. I'll have you there in ten minutes."

"Thanks."

A big sign outside the mall listed the names of some of the shops inside, so I could go straight to the one I needed instead of suffering through a hit-and-miss.

"Drop me off at JC Penny. It would be cool if you would wait."

I bought a pair of Levi's, three pairs of underwear, shorts, socks, a button-down navy blue shirt to wear out and three T-shirts. I had so much at home that it felt sinful to buy what I was buying.

At the hotel, the bellman wanted to help with my two small bags. I thanked him and kept going to the entrance. I was feeling better and becoming interested in Donna. Walking through the casino, I noticed the action at the blackjack tables. One table had an empty seat to the left of the dealer.

I stopped.

The dealer was in the middle of a hand. I put both bags on the floor between my legs and reached in my pocket. I didn't want to sit down, so I didn't count the cash. I took about half the roll without making a big deal of it and placed it on the table.

The dealer asked for bets.

"Money plays," I said. I knew he would count it.

"Money plays. Five thousand two hundred."

The pit boss repeated, "Money plays. Five thousand two hundred."

I was fucking crazy. I picked up the bags with one hand and had already decided I would walk away if I won or lost. The dealer had seventeen. I stayed on twenty.

The table clapped.

"Give me five hundred chips, please."

I placed a hundred-dollar bill and pointed for him to take it. He smiled and tapped the bill on the table, then put it in his shirt pocket.

I returned the cash to my pocket and scooped up the five thousand two hundred in chips to another pocket.

"I'd stay, but I have a guest waiting for me," I said and waved goodbye.

I called that a hit-and-run. If I was a whistler, I would have whistled all the way to my suite.

When I walked into the suite, I saw Donna's back against the backdrop of the floor-to-ceiling windows. Shining against the darkness of the strip were the lights of the Dunes Hotel, the Riviera, the Moulin Rouge, and a vacant darkness between the Tropicana and the Dunes. Above downtown Las Vegas, where I had played at the Fremont Hotel, was a distant glare in the sky.

Donna turned from the view as I set the bags on a chair. The hotel robe all but swallowed her up.

"Did you find what you needed?"

"I did," I said. "How's the wine?"

"Delicious."

She dropped the robe and opened her arms like Elena might have done. I hugged her. She undressed me while my hands were busy on her body.

Nude, I took my jeans with me to the master bath and, except for two hundred dollars, put the cash and chips in the safe. I put the two hundred in my jeans pocket, showered, and came out through the bedroom on my way to the living room bar to prepare a CC water.

Donna was a slow drinker.

"Try the wine," she said. "Let me pour you some."

I discarded the idea of Canadian Club and went for the wine. Donna had the bottle in the bedroom. Convenient. We clicked.

"You're right. It's good," I said.

As if she knew me, she said, "Sip it slowly, G. Enjoy it."

"You know wines?"

"I am learning," she said. "This one is very good."

"I agree," I said.

* * *

I didn't call Elena, and she didn't call me.

I was suddenly pissed off at Elena for leaving me because I was becoming a drunk like Ramirez.

* * *

That night was like the first night with a girlfriend, but it was not awkward. I don't think Donna had been in the business long, though I don't remember why I thought that. Maybe because she was younger than me or my age. She wasn't a boozer. She was rather classy and a real blonde. She kept her eyes open when we kissed. She kept her eyes open when I was on top of her, her legs raised above her head, our faces inches apart. In that moment between total strangers, she was irresistible, and no talking was necessary. I held on until Donna was about to orgasm. Her position changed. She got on her side, the sex became feral, and she screamed. I don't believe she was faking.

When we were drenched with sweat and starving, I ordered a Porterhouse steak, and Donna ordered a salad and a small pizza. Room service served it in the suite's dining room, a high-gloss black enamel table that reminded me of one of our paint jobs at the shop.

"So, what do you do besides this?"

"For now, all I do is this," she said. "What do you do?"

"I hustle every day to keep my business alive," I said.

"Your own boss, huh? How do you score a suite like this? Are you paying for it?"

"If I lose, I'm paying for it."

She stared at me. "I feel like I've known you for a long time."

"I thought the same thing when we were in bed."

She offered me a bite of pizza. My hands were full with the giant Porterhouse, but I took a nibble.

"I shouldn't say this while we're eating," she said.

"Tell me anything. It's okay."

"I came twice." Her smile was great!

I reached over and touched her face.

"Was it good?"

"It was better than good," she said. "Thank you."

"My pleasure," I said.

* * *

We both slept until ten. I couldn't remember when I'd slept that late. Donna stayed until noon, and I didn't jog. Fuck it. I needed to be away. No wonder Elena was gone. I wore her out. I figured she wouldn't last at the shop. Leaving the house was just her first move. She'd quit soon. Nothing lasts forever. My first wife, Selena, told me that.

I gave Donna two hundred dollars.

"Is that enough?"

Donna kissed me.

"It's plenty," she said.

Girls in her business, do they say that? I handed her my business card.

"If you're ever in Los Angeles, call me."

"I will. Are you out of here today?"

"Not sure yet."

"G, if you don't leave, I'll be in the bar tonight."

We kissed, and she was gone.

I showered and put on my same pair of jeans. I liked the faded look better than the new ones. I wore the button-down shirt I bought.

I went straight to the cashier and got cash for the chips. I felt like it was bad luck to take a win from the night before to a table. I was lucky when I played with green cash.

Here's what I did differently: I played and lost two thousand. Instead of sticking it out, I changed tables. I seldom change tables. I lost a thousand right off at the second table but stuck it out. Two hours or so later, I walked away from that table with almost fifty thousand dollars.

My host showed up. You'd think he'd be mad because I won, but that was not the case.

"Stay another night," he urged. "I have the suite booked for you."

I shook hands with Jimmy and handed him two hundred.

"Thanks, I think I'll take you up on that," I said.

"Can I call you George?"

"Of course," I said.

"If you need anything, call me. They'll page me. I'll get right back to you. Anything, George."

"Got it," I said. We shook hands.

"Want me to set you up with check cashing or credit?"

I didn't want to sound lame and ask what that was.

"If I do, I'll be on you in no time," I said. "Thanks for the offer."

* * *

I figured I had the money I had when I arrived plus fifty thousand or so. I wanted to call Elena and give her the good news but didn't. I never called Mike or my other guys at the shops. I was happy to stay the night and happier when I found Donna in the bar drinking a virgin margarita.

"Hi, G. Are you looking for a date?"

"Not anymore," I said. "How about dinner? Where do you want to go?"

"I think we could be cozy in the suite with a nice bottle of wine. I'm still full from last night."

"All you ate was a salad."

"And the pizza and the bowl of ice cream?"

"You know, you're really beautiful," I said.

She blushed. "I love your hair," she whispered. "I love that." She pointed at my fly.

"I wouldn't say you are beautiful if I didn't mean it."

"If I'm so beautiful, why do only the old guys ask me up to their room?"

"The younger ones are busy working, so they can afford to be here."

Donna laughed.

"I like you, G. Did you have a good day?"

"I did. I have enough so I can give you deuce again."

"Bitchin'," she said.

We started toward the elevator. I reached in my pocket, pulled out two hundred dollars, stopped at the first table that had a vacant chair, and set the two hundred on the table. We stood next to each other.

"Money plays," I said.

The pit boss repeated, and the dealer dealt the cards. I stayed on twenty. The dealer had nineteen. I pushed the two hundred cash and chips forward.

The dealer said, "Four hundred plays."

I got twelve and didn't hit. The dealer busted. I took eight hundred from the table.

"I'll be back," I said.

"Man, you are lucky. Is that the way you play?"

"Donna, that was your money I played. This is yours," I said.

Her eyes grew wide. We stopped walking. People cascaded all around us.

"Is that bitchin' or what?" She put the cash and chips in her purse. "G, you will not be able to walk tomorrow when I'm done with you tonight."

We were walking again. "It's you who won't be able to walk."

"That would be wonderful," she said.

It was like a second date with a girlfriend. A pretty lady I was lucky to hook up with. I would have been lonely that night without her. The host had hinted he would fix me up, but I didn't need fixing. I already knew Donna. I should have been totally happy with the money I'd won. Maybe I was, but it was a strange time for me, what with Elena leaving me.

In the morning, Donna gave me the phone number of a hotel two blocks away where she'd been living for two months. "I'm not going anywhere. Leave a message, and I'll call you back," she said.

"I don't even know your last name," I said.

"Jenkins. Donna Jenkins."

"I gave you my card yesterday. Call me."

"I might surprise you," she said.

I packed up my purchases and laundry in a fancy hotel shopping bag, left a message for the host thanking him for all the attention and the great wine, called the front desk, and told them I was leaving. I headed downstairs, not tempted to stop at a table on my way out. I would roll the dice about catching a plane. The airport was tiny, and everything was in one building. I boarded on the tarmac.

One thing about the airport is the same. Plenty of slot machines.

George Hatcher

Chapter 4
Back To Reality

At LAX, it cost me twenty dollars for two and a half days of parking. I skipped going to the house or apartment. It was a workday, Friday, two in the afternoon when I got to the shop. No one was parked in my spot. Elena's spot was empty. She probably walked from her aunt's house.

As I walked toward the entrance, I saw Elena and Susie, both with customers. Elena looked up from her clipboard, cast me a tiny surprised look, and then flashed the smile I loved so much.

"Hi," I said, loud enough for Elena and Susie to hear, and walked directly up to my office.

Elena had made the bank deposits already. The receipts, including the Soto shop deposits that Gil managed, were sorted and done. The money from Soto came over every day, and we handled preparing the deposit. Mike did his own. There was nothing for me to do. The invoices were already in the desk tray for Donald when he came in.

My desk was clean.

I emptied my pockets on the top of my desk, finding a five-hundred-dollar chip that I forgot to cash in with my two bundles of cash. I counted out nine thousand two hundred in hundreds. Eight thousand came from Rene's. The balance was the money I had on me. I set the ninety-two hundred on the side and started counting the other money.

Elena walked in.

"Hey, stranger. You didn't call. I was beginning to worry about you."

I stopped counting and looked up.

"You knew I was staying at Flamingo."

"I called three times, but there was no answer in your room, and I didn't leave a message with the desk."

"I'm sorry. I kept busy."

"Fuck, you won!"

I had the stack of uncounted cash in my hand. She saw the pile on the desk first, then what was in my hand.

"I did. Come help me count. This is the money I went up with," I touched the nine thousand two hundred pile.

"This is what I won." I held up the rest.

"And like always, you stuff it all in your jeans pockets."

I got up.

"I gotta pee, be back."

I was going to pass her when she stopped me. She grabbed my crotch and moved me toward her.

"No kiss? Nothing for Elena?"

We kissed, a wet one. It was lacking something.

"Be back," I said.

When I returned, she said, "Fifty-eight thousand one hundred dollars."

"I didn't go up to win again. I mean, I always want to win, but it wasn't a live-or-die thing as in the past. If I had lost, I would have been another nine-thousand-two hundred in the hole. But I needed to get away, and that's why I went up."

"You did good, G."

Before I said anything, I dialed Rene's Check Cashing to tell him he didn't need to hold the check for eight thousand. He could deposit. "Put the winnings in the safe. I'll run to the bank and deposit the money to cover Rene."

"What's the rush? The check won't be at the bank for days."

I nodded. "Yeah, you're right. I'm tired. Do me a favor. Put the money in the safe. I'm going home." I took twelve hundred and put it in my pocket.

"Which home?"

"The apartment."

I didn't hug and kiss Elena or thank her for taking care of business while I was gone. I walked past her and down the stairs. Instead of a thank you, I was short with words and ignored her pass when she grabbed and kissed me.

Before going out to the car, I caught Susie without a customer and gave her a hug.

"All good?"

"All good, Jefe. Did you have fun?"

I winked and gave her a thumbs-up.

"Are you working tomorrow?" she asked.

"It's Saturday. I may surprise everyone and stay home."

I blew her a kiss.

* * *

I stopped at the grocery store and bought the usual odds and ends: crackers, cheese, peanut butter, two kinds of jelly, bread, bagels, cream cheese, coffee, paper plates, paper cups, napkins, and bachelor stuff. I went back for ice cream.

I stopped at the liquor store on Floral, a high-end big place that catered to the homes in Monterey Hills, mostly people in the middle and upper money-earning class.

"I had a French Merlot in Vegas last night I really liked," I told the man behind the counter.

"I have French Merlots, but there are many to choose from." He led me to a section of the store and pointed out the wall of Merlots. "You didn't get a name?"

"No, it's okay. I'll take three of these." I went by the higher price. Fifteen dollars a bottle was a lot of money, considering that a quart of Canadian Club was less than three dollars. I knew my supply of CC was low, but it didn't matter. I didn't buy any. I was going to switch to a slow high with wine.

I drove to the apartment, turned on the television, stretched out on the sofa by the phone, and called Mike at his house.

"So, Elena packed and left," I said, looking straight ahead at a film of dust on the television screen.

"I called the shop, and she answered the phone twice today."

"She left me, not the shop. She's working, but she split. Her clothes are gone. Anyway, I'm at the apartment." I leaned over the side table and blew on it. Dust flew. Not an insane amount, but enough to make me sneeze.

"Sorry, brother."

"Use your key to my pad. As soon as I hang up, go feed the fish for me."

"I fed them yesterday. I'll do it right off. I didn't know what was going on, but I took care of it. Don't worry about them. Fuckers won't let me pet them, but they have no problem eating the flakes I feed them."

"Thanks, Mike. I'm going to get the guy who cleans the tank for me to move them back to the apartment."

"Don't rush it, brother. She'll be back. Don't worry about the fish."

"Thanks."

"Love you, bro."

"Ditto." I pictured Mike grinning

The apartment was looking rough. I didn't need to white-finger all the surfaces. In my living room, I saw dust on the TV and tables. I got two terry cleaning towels and lemon oil from the laundry room. Cleaning reminded me of my janitor days. I wished I could whistle while I worked my way through the entire apartment, dusting. While I was cleaning, I found Elena's front door key on top of the small dining table. I dusted around it but didn't touch it. I ran water in the kitchen, turned on the garbage disposal, and let it run. I took a used lemon, dropped it in, and soon I could smell the freshness.

It took almost an hour to clean up and change the sheets. When I'd moved out of the apartment, I had left behind practically everything except for clothes. I had a ridiculous amount of tennis shoes here, plus some unused locker stuff. The lady decorator had stocked the house, so the bedding was not as good as some of my locker thing stuff. The apartment was home. Fuck the house. I wasn't sure if I missed Elena, who had abandoned me, or Donna, who I'd left in Las Vegas.

I looked around for a corkscrew, and I realized I didn't own one.

I dialed.

Ava answered.

"Hey, hope I'm not disturbing you."

"G – what a surprise," Ava said. "Are you at the new house or here?"

"I'm here. Going to be for a while."

"She with you?"

"Her name is Elena."

"Oops, sorry."

"Don't be. Hey, I need a corkscrew, and I don't own one."

"I'll bring it over."

Ava knocked two minutes later as I got to the door. She was in a pair of red short shorts, strappy high heels that looked impossible to walk in, a red choker, and a string top that didn't leave a whole lot to the imagination, but as far as my imagination was concerned, that was a gift.

"I'd forgotten how hot you look," I said.

She gave me a dangerous look. "How dare you. I'm so insulted." She took a step toward me, wrapped her hands around my waist, and gave me a stunning Ava-kiss.

I needed the kiss I got.

We stayed close. The kiss continued with my arms around her. Eventually, we came up for air and just looked at each other. I admit my hands may strayed down to her fine ass.

"G, I wish I could stay," she said. "I have someone coming over any minute."

She handed me the corkscrew. It had a blonde wood handle, with the metal corkscrew stuck into the middle of it so that it resembled a 'T.' There wasn't a moving part to eject the cork off the screw, but I figured I could just wind it down.

"We got plenty of them. Keep it."

"Thanks," I said and kissed her. "Too bad you got to rush. Have a good night."

And she was gone. I didn't ask about Emma.

I went to the kitchen, got a knife out of a drawer, and cut the foil as Donna had done, then I opened the bottle. Screwing the corkscrew into the cork was a piece of cake, and so was pulling it out of the bottle. It took me an extra second to figure out how to wind the cork off the screw. I left the cork on the counter and let the wine breathe for about five minutes while I changed into shorts and a t-shirt. I went to the console I used as a bar and grabbed one of the highball glasses Elena and I used for CC water.

I would have to buy wine glasses if I switched over from CC.

I turned the TV on and lowered the volume all the way so I could hear the tunes from my record player. The house had a new hi-fi much classier than the one here. I sat on one of my comfy chairs and sipped the wine. Truth be told, I didn't know if it was the same, better, or worse than what I'd had in Vegas. I did like the smoothness of it, and it tasted better than Canadian Club.

I picked up the wine bottle and looked at it. The guy at Salud Liquor selling the wine recommended Pomeroy Merlot. Donna had said Merlot came from dark grapes. If I hadn't been so busy having sex with her, I could have quizzed her about wine, but she was too young to be much of an expert. I didn't like that the wine left my tongue stained. Even brushing with a toothbrush doesn't get it all off.

I did something I rarely do. I dozed off in the chair, my empty glass on the table by me. The phone rang, waking me up. I didn't get up fast enough, and it stopped ringing. It rang again a second time when I was brushing my tongue, and that time, I got it.

"What are you doing?" Elena asked, sounding way too cheerful.

"I passed out in the chair watching TV and listening to tunes, and no, I wasn't drunk."

"Baby, don't be like that."

I sighed. "I'm sorry."

"You miss me?"

* * *

I was putting on my tennis shoes for the morning jog when I opened the door. There she was, in white shorts and a T-shirt like mine but smaller.

"Morning, baby," she said.

In the open doorway, I kissed her, hugged her, held her close.

"Morning," I said.

That morning, had I not been married, I was ripe for the picking. If Elena had agreed, I would have married her so that I'd never lose her. I know what you're thinking. Insecurity, big time.

We didn't run to the top of the hill. Our jog was purposely slow and level, so it was easier for me to talk.

"If I don't generate more cash flow, it's all going to fall apart."

"What's the plan?"

I slowed down, stopped, and turned to look at her. She ran past me, then stopped to look back.

"Stay tuned," I said, running but not charging ahead.

"Uh, oh," Elena said.

I told her about liking the Merlot in Vegas and how I bought some at Salud Liquor last night. "I need to buy wine glasses."

"I drank wine in Hawaii," Elena said. "The Texan had a huge wine cellar filled with hundreds of bottles of wine. When he was away, I'd spend way too much time down there, drinking like there was no tomorrow. The couple who worked there as custodians told me the wine was worth a fortune. Wine is just as bad as Canadian Club."

"I don't know about that," I said. "I'm going to drink wine moderately."

"Who turned you on to wine?"

I told her without hesitation, "I got comped. I got a suite like we got twice before. It had a wine cooler stocked with wine."

"Sounds like you did more than gamble."

"I can't lie," I said. "I kicked back. You would like this girl."

"I would like this girl?" Elena said with a laugh, kind of sarcastic.

"Well, she's very nice. Her name is Donna."

Elena ignored what I said. "Baby, one of these days, you will lose."

"Not if I don't go back."

"You promised before."

"I know."

When we got to the apartment, she went down to her car for a change of clothes.

"No need," I said. "It's Saturday. I'm not going in."

"I know Susie can handle it," Elena said after she came out of the shower. "And if Alexa is with her, for sure, they can handle a Saturday. I think I need to be there. The cow needs love and care that only you and I can provide."

She left me speechless. I stayed home, and Elena left for the shop.

I showered and dressed. I looked through the classifieds. I made coffee, drank a cup, washed the mug I drank it in, washed the glass from last night. I ran out of things to keep my mind off the shop. I lasted less than an hour after she left. I drove to the shop. As I pulled into the parking lot with my window rolled down, Elena did that whistle she can do (and which I can't.)

She was sitting on a bench we have near the entrance, stood up when she saw me and clapped like I had done one of those crazy dives from a mountaintop like she told me she'd seen in Hawaii. Susie did too. I had to laugh. It was probably the first time I had a standing ovation like that since I took that drama class in school.

I was overwhelmed with emotion, though no one could see my tears. Only I truly understood the depth of what I felt, and there was no question that the stress had brought me to that state. Decades have passed, and yet those feelings remain. I always knew it was unrealistic to believe that the Vegas wins would keep coming. The influx of money from Vegas was what sustained everything; it wasn't just my shop that I referred to as the cash cow.

* * *

Judge Teran, a friend of Judge Black, was a Superior Court Judge at the downtown courthouse. Judge Teran called to say that he was sending his wife's station wagon. He wanted all nicks and dents repaired, a taillight housing replaced, and the car painted its original color.

"No rush. We have plenty of cars. We can get by without the wagon."

"No problem, Judge. Send it over."

Judge T sent a couple of marshals to drop the wagon at the shop.

Donald insisted every car had to have an invoice, so I wrote out an invoice with no price. If I decided not to charge the customer, I'd write it on the invoice, and he'd take care of it, whatever that meant.

A week later, I told the judge I would mail him an invoice, but I didn't plan to charge him. Judge T sent a T-Bird, a beautiful 1957 that reminded me how much I loved that model. He wanted the original paint job on that one too. These were not thirty-five-dollar jobs. They took time to prepare and to apply color coats. That means the painter paints the car one time, and it doesn't even need the oven. It's lacquer paint that dries fast. The sander waits a day or two, then re-sands the car, the masking tape is replaced, and the painter shoots it again. Depending on how the second coat comes out, it might end there, or a third coat might be applied after it is sanded again. Finally, when it's finished, a painter's helper buffs the car using a rubbing compound. The car was picked up, and like Judge Black had done the first time, Judge T called to find out why he had not received an invoice.

"I will send it, Judge, don't worry about it too much."

Judge Teran wanted to take me to lunch. I agreed. He came to the shop and picked me up himself, and he chose a steak house on Olympic Boulevard that I didn't even know was there. It had great steaks. I have this to say about Judge Teran. Not all judges look like judges. Some of them, when they take off the robe, their dignity goes with it. Judge Teran looked like a judge, no matter what he was wearing. He had that air of power, dignity, and wisdom.

"I owe you, young man," he said when he dropped me off.

"No, Judge, you don't owe me. I'm here for anything you need."

He was ready to drive off. I was already out of the car and talking to him through the open window.

"You're going to do great things one day," he told me in Spanish.

We would become good friends.

* * *

The student who looked after my fish moved the tank and the fish to my apartment and installed them where I'd had them before. It took him all of eight hours to do this. It took two days for my fish to adjust and get over their apparent anger at being tossed around. Who knew fish could be so temperamental? They refused to eat and ignored me when I tried to pet them.

Mike suggested I rent the house out. So did Elena.

I got the house for Elena, and she was suggesting I rent it out.

Okay, it is true that I wanted that house. I wanted to wake up in that house. I wanted to go to bed at night in that house. I wanted to wade in the lap pool bare-ass naked if that's what I wanted to do.

I decided to keep it as is. I moved all my clothes back to my apartment. It was difficult to give up the great walk-in closets for standard slider door closets, but that's what I did.

Elena showed up once in a while but never unannounced, and we both accepted the different terms. One time when the doorbell rang, I was with Emma in bed. I put on my skivvies and walked to the front door slowly for my pecker to settle down.

Elena no longer had a key.

Elena was just walking away when I opened the door. I was standing in my skivvies early on a Sunday afternoon with people in the pool looking at me. It didn't faze me in the least.

"Hi," she said with a little wave. "I called, but no answer. Took a chance you'd be here."

I was going to tell her I was busy, but she had to know that.

"Can I come in and wait?"

"Elena, come in."

Her eyes were red like she'd been crying. I could see pearls of tears on her lashes, and her eyes were moist.

I extended my hand to her, and she walked inside.

Seconds later, Emma stepped into the living room dressed in shorts, a teaser top, and sandals.

"I was just leaving," she lied.

We'd just been at it big time.

"Good to see you. Elena, miss you," Emma said.

They kissed.

Emma left.

I was standing there. Elena was a foot away from the front door.

I opened my arms. Elena dropped her purse on the floor, openly crying.

I swept her into a hug.

"I can't do this anymore," she said. "I want to be with you, and not only at work."

* * *

We didn't want the house anymore. After we came to that agreement, an employee of her aunt, a mortician, drove out with Elena to see the house. That afternoon he wrote me a check for the months I had left that I had prepaid. I accepted half of what I had paid for the furniture and all the trimmings.

"I'm convinced you can sell anything," I told Elena that night.

"The house sold itself. Lorenzo loves it. He fell in love with every room, even the empty bedroom where you had planned to put in a gym. He plans to put an office there. I won't be surprised if he buys it."

"He doesn't look like an undertaker," I said.

"Baby, he's a licensed funeral director. He doesn't do that for my aunt, but he's an embalmer. One day he'll open his own place. My aunt says he's good."

I teased her. "What does good mean?"

"Oh, stop," she laughed and shoved me.

I kissed her. "Do me a favor," I said.

"Anything."

"Let me give you the check he gave me. It's yours."

"Baby, no."

"I want you to go buy a big box of new lingerie," I said.

"I have way too much; you know that. I said no."

I got her to accept the check. It took two days.

If I had put the check in my bank, overhead would have eaten it up. I wanted to give her something big, but the timing was off.

One night, we were nestled against a mountain of pillows in bed, the soft glow of the television casting flickering shadows on the walls. The room was filled with the comforting hum of our favorite show, a familiar escape from the chaos of the world outside. Suddenly, Elena turned to me, her eyes searching mine with an intensity that made my heart skip a beat.

"Am I prettier than the girl in Vegas?" she asked, her voice tinged with a mix of curiosity and insecurity.

I chuckled softly, trying to lighten the mood. "What girl?"

"You mentioned her name is Donna. If she's a hooker, that's probably not her real name, but just tell me—is she a knockout?"

"Baby, don't label her like that," I said gently, feeling a

pang of guilt. "She hustles just like Emma and Ava. Calling her a hooker feels so demeaning."

Before Elena could respond, I wrapped my arm around her and pulled her close, our faces inches apart. I kissed her, my lips lingering on hers, trying to convey all the love and reassurance I felt. "I love you," I whispered against her mouth.

A little later that night, as the room grew quieter and the show faded into the background, Elena broke the silence. "Our love is wicked," she said, her voice barely above a whisper. "We share your bed with Susie. I fucked Mike, and you have a girlfriend in Donna. What else do we both have going on?"

"I thought we wanted it that way," I replied, my voice steady but my mind racing.

There was a long silence, punctuated only by the sound of our breathing. Finally, she sighed deeply, a sound filled with resignation and acceptance. "You're right. We want each other, but we want to be free."

At that moment, the weight of our unconventional love settled over us like a heavy blanket, both comforting and suffocating. We lay there, tangled in each other's arms, knowing that our love was as complicated as it was passionate and that we were bound by a desire for both connection and freedom.

Thanks to Elena, I learned more about wine. Sunday, we drove out to West Los Angeles to buy the wine she remembered liking at the Texan's house. We both were drinking a little wine every day, slowly to savor it. I said goodbye to the Canadian Club. I didn't expect to ever go back to drinking it in the future.

* * *

One Friday night, we went out to dinner in Hollywood. For a change, we were suited up. Elena wore a gorgeous black dress with a laced-up waist, polished high heels, and a matching purse. The restaurant was on top of a high-rise with a spectacular view.

The waiter sent us the wine steward.

"We're starting out with wine," I said. "Actually, I'm starting out. Elena here knows her way around, but not me. We like Pomeroy Merlot. We're thinking of broadening our horizons and trying something other than Merlot tonight."

Pages of Passion Book 4: Threads of Destiny

Elena

He went through a bunch of wines. Elena was attentive to what he said.

"Baby let's try the Chateau Margaux," she said. "It's French like Pomeroy. I think you'll like it."

"Let's do it," I agreed.

The wine steward bunched the fingers of his right hand to his mouth and smacked.

"Baby, you continue to impress me," I said.

"If we get tipsy, we take a taxi. Deal?"

"Of course," I said. "We take the bottle home."

She looked happy to hear that.

No matter what you ordered, if it was baked, grilled, or served on a plate in any condition other than raw, to make it really fancy, it was flamed table-side to make it magical. That's what they did to our NY Peppercorn Steak Diane.

I loved Elena, but because we had steak, I did have a picture of Donna in Las Vegas float through my mind. I'd had a porterhouse with her for a late dinner. What a night that had been, and we didn't get up until ten am.

The restaurant's view of nighttime Los Angeles was incomparable. The delicious steaks were buttery, mustardy, savory, and melt-in-your-mouth tender. I was falling in love with wine, and the wine Elena suggested was fantastic.

"What's to become of us?" I asked.

Elena looked across the small table at me. We were seated next to a wall of floor-to-ceiling windows, and, of course, that view.

"What do you mean?"

"I mean, what's to become of us?"

"We're going to be together for a long time," she said, raising her glass and holding it out towards me. We clicked.

"Is marriage in the plan?" It was a dummy question, and I knew it before I said it.

"Baby, there's no plan. It's us. You and me."

I didn't say anything. I went blank. I do that.

"Baby, marriage would mean no freedom like we both want."

I raised my glass to hers. "You're right," I said.

Her words reminded me of Selena, who had once said the same thing—not quite the same thing, but close.

My mouth agreed. My brain was on the fence.

All the way home, Elena had at least one of her hands on me, mostly in my hair. When we got in the car, the radio was playing loud. She had turned the volume down early on. Me, I like it loud, but in the car, she didn't go for it.

"I think you and I are not made to be married to each other or anyone," Elena said.

"You say that because we do it with Susie? Because I bedded Donna in Vegas?"

"I never asked you how many times did you see her?"

"At least twice," I said.

"I'm no angel either, baby."

"Yeah, you are," I teased.

"I fucked Mike," she said. "Almost fucked him again, but he got cold on me."

"What?"

She laughed. "I'm kidding, baby."

Several seconds passed. "Baby, did you almost fuck him?"

A few seconds later. "He got cold on me. Turned me down."

"Wow," I said. I was going to ask for details but I didn't. I was proud of Mike. Did she ask him?

"Don't be mad, G. Nothing happened."

After a short pause, I said, "Hey, we're free to do what we want."

I drove for a few miles with no conversation, nothing but the radio. I had to ask.

"But you'd fuck him again?"

"Baby, he turned me down."

"I see what you mean about marriage," I said.

"You sound like a victim."

I knew she was teasing, but she'd hit a nerve.

"No, I'm not a victim. One thing is a sure thing. You are the most special woman in my life."

"I am right now. Time will tell for how long." She wound her fingers in my hair and tugged.

"I don't want to think that you would leave again," I said.

"I'm with you all the way," she said.

It didn't happen immediately.

Just after we'd finished a long jog, Elena said, "I'm going on a trip to Hawaii. I won't be that long. You have Susie and Alexa. Is that okay?"

"Baby, I don't own you. Why you ask if it's okay?"

"Because I want you to be okay with it."

We were getting dressed for work. She had not mentioned this during our run.

"You're going there to see David Marks, that old Texan. When you going?"

"This afternoon. I'm going to pack and take a taxi to the airport."

"Why taxi? You have a car."

It was a stupid statement.

"I'm leaving it here. I don't trust LAX parking."

I set my coffee cup on the nightstand, laced my tennis, and walked to the closet for a t-shirt. I put back the T-shirt and picked out a navy blue button-down shirt that I'd never worn before. All the buttons to the top were buttoned. As I unbuttoned, I said, "I can't think of anything you'd be pissed about," I said.

"I'm not pissed," she said. "I need to spring out for a little bit, okay?"

"Absolutely," I said. "Go to Hawaii. Will you call me?"

"Absolutely," she said with a half giggle.

"Okay, you spring to Hawaii. I'll spring to the shop."

We hugged and kissed.

"I love you," she said.

"Ditto," I said as I walked out of the bedroom.

I didn't get pissed off until I was driving to the shop. She was free, and I was free.

She was right that marriage was not right for us. I was going to do some springing of my own.

Chapter 5
Judy's Brother Leonard

On the morning that Elena left, my son Leonard Hatcher was born.

During one of those rare visits to see my daughter Judy, Sophia and I found a moment alone. We slipped into the bedroom, and before we knew it, she became pregnant. Surprised? That was the reason the divorce hadn't happened yet. We had agreed to wait until after the baby was born. Neither Elena nor Mike knew about Sophia's pregnancy.

George Hatcher

Sophia

It was clear that Sophia's entire army of a family had nothing but disgust for me. I knew it, they knew I knew it, and Sophia knew it too. No one bothered to call me until after the baby was born, and Sophia was already at the hospital. She named him Leonard, after my stepdad, which was great. I don't recall being consulted about a name for a boy or girl. That's what happens when you're a distant husband; the fault was my own.

Wearing my new button-down shirt instead of my usual t-shirt felt like I had dressed for the occasion. I paid my visit to the hospital to kiss Sophia, congratulate her, and check out my son, who was a good looker from the start. I waved at the family crowd but don't remember shaking any hands. Before leaving, I went to the cashier and paid the balance due to the hospital, having already paid a deposit months before.

When I came back to the shop, everyone stopped working for a little while to clap and cheer. Susie and Alexa even kissed me. Elena was probably on a plane over the Pacific Ocean. Mike called, wanting to go out that night to celebrate.

"I can't drink and drive," I said, "but hey, your call means a lot to me."

"Brother, did you buy any cigars?" he asked.

"The only place around here that has them is the liquor store, and those are the cheap sticks that Ramirez smoked."

"Vicki is at work. I told her about the baby. She sends her congratulations and hugs."

"Give her a hug for me. Tell her I miss her."

"Hey, Bro, you rented the place to an undertaker. I didn't know that when I met him."

"He's a good guy," I said. "We're all going to need an undertaker someday. Be nice."

"I'm going to pretend you didn't say that, brother."

Before heading to my apartment, I went by the hospital again. I looked in on Sophia. She was asleep. The nurse told me she was fine and would be discharged the next afternoon. I stopped by to see the baby through the glass window.

"Leonie, you a good-looking kiddo. Daddy loves you," I said aloud. No one heard me, but I think Leonie moved when I said that.

On my way home, I thought about stopping for food or going to eat-in somewhere, but I kept driving. I had lots of crackers and three different kinds of cheese, and good wine. I wondered why I hadn't asked Susie over. There was always tomorrow.

I laid out the cheese and a handful of crackers on a chopping block. It was a messy spread, nothing like Elena would fix for us. She was always adding nuts and fruit that only she shopped for because I forgot the odds and ends.

I poured a nip of Bordeaux. I had a variety to choose from, all of them from France. I was still at a point in my wine education where I liked everything I tried. The nip tasted good. I turned on the music. The TV was already on. I took another nip of wine. A nip is a tiny bit, a little less than what a wine steward gives you in a restaurant to have you try out the wine you ordered.

I think Elena, deep down, really liked Ava and Emma, but sometimes she said something that made me believe otherwise.

"You have a sticky relationship with them, baby. They are with who knows how many men, and you take them to bed like it's nothing."

"I haven't taken them to bed since you've been back."

I called my neighbors. Ava was busy, but Emma was free. Emma appeared at my door thirty minutes later. She smelled great to me, as she always did. Whenever we had been in bed, I smelled the perfume, My Sin, that I had given her and Ava. I had a bag of it from the locker thing. Alicia and Clara had kept most of it.

"Are you staying all night?"

"Is Elena coming over?"

"She's not," I said.

Emma hugged me tight and wrapped her legs around me.

"I'm staying all night."

Sometime later, the phone rang, but I didn't answer. A little later, the phone rang again. Probably Elena.

Chapter 6
Money Was Always Scarce

No question, I was good at cashing checks to float shortages. I had three other check-cashing places in addition to Chester and Rene, all hungry to make the juice cashing checks for me, depositing right away or holding them for extra juice. My desktop-sized planner had the name of each check-cashing place, and below each, a check amount and date. When I covered the check at the bank, I'd cross it off. Most of the time, when I crossed it off, a new check elsewhere covered the one I crossed off. Sounds complicated, but to me, it wasn't. It was the same as getting eight thousand from Chester and eventually telling him to deposit the check I had given him so he could get his bosses' money back.

Donald said, "Your payrolls have doubled."

"Business has doubled," I insisted.

"I don't see it. George, the service charges you are paying the check cashers are getting heavier and heavier, and that percentage Sam is getting may be your profit where Mike is."

He called it services charges. I called it juice.

* * *

The first call I got from Elena that I answered was at the shop.

"Baby, I've been gone for four days and haven't been able to reach you. Didn't Susie give you my phone number?"

"Hey," I said, ignoring what she said. "I miss you, baby."

"Congratulations. Susie told me you had a boy. That's totally wonderful, baby," she said brightly. "Are you happy?"

"Yeah, happy, of course. He's a looker. Going to kill the ladies."

"Like his daddy."

I pictured Susie on top of me last night. "Yeah, like his daddy," I said, laughing. "Hey, I've been overwhelmed with alligators and rattlers. Sorry I didn't get back to you. I figured I'd give you space."

"G did I miss something? I didn't know your wife was pregnant."

"I must have told you," I lied. "That's why I haven't gotten the divorce. We agreed to wait until the baby was born."

"Okay," she said.

A minute later we were done talking.

Sophia and I had a number of excuses for delaying the divorce that went way back before we learned she was pregnant. The current reason was waiting for her to give birth.

Elena hadn't been gone a week when I took off to Vegas, hoping to make a killing and cut the float totally or by a huge chunk. I was afraid to add it up.

I cashed the eight-thousand-dollar check at Rene's, and he agreed to hold the check for three days. That gave me at least seven banking days to cover it when I got back.

I was going to call Donna, but it was a good thing I didn't. In less than an hour, I lost the eight thousand and headed back home. I wasn't even pissed off. I was giving back their money. Of course, I had already used my winnings, so what I just lost put me in the hole big time.

Fuck it.

To cover the eight-thousand-dollar check I'd given Rene, I cashed a check for the same amount at another check cashing place. I covered Rene's check, and now I had to cover the new check I'd written for the cash I'd put in the bank to cover that eight thousand dollars.

* * *

By the time Tuesday night arrived, I felt battered. The loss in Vegas and the relentless pressure to run and cover checks were driving me crazy. I had planned to spend the evening with both Ava and Emma. To avoid complaints from their unscrupulous pimp about them not working, I agreed to pay him his cut. In the past, I had intervened when he was beating Ava, which led to me hurting him. As a result, he didn't trust me and didn't want to see me again. The arrangement was clear: I wouldn't interact with him directly. Instead, I would hand the money to the girls, and they would pass it on to him.

With both of them there, the bed was on fire. I didn't drink, and neither did they. It was animal sex. I needed animal sex. This kind of sex would be the trend later in the seventies. The addiction doesn't last forever.

In the morning, I took care of the girls, and I gave them the hundred dollars for the pimp.

No matter how busy I was the morning after Ava and Emma, the heat of the bed the night before played in my brain. It was savage

Pages of Passion Book 4: Threads of Destiny

* * *

My biggest regret about going to Vegas was that I didn't manage to hook up with Donna. I thought about calling her and making a deal for her to come to see me for a weekend. I'd pay her airfare and anything else plus her services, but then there was Susie.

I've always disliked being alone; it goes back ages. Yet, I've been lucky—there's usually someone around to keep me company. Before Elena left, she mentioned I had Susie and Alexa as though she was trying to fix me up. She didn't even acknowledge Ava and Emma, who live across the hall, Letty from the pizza parlor down the street, or Donna in Las Vegas. Sure, they're all great in their own way, but Susie? She's truly special.

Susie was a breath of fresh air. On Friday night, her laughter filled my apartment as we cooked dinner together. The next morning, we shared the drive to work, the warm aroma of fresh coffee making the ride even better. She returned to my place Saturday afternoon, her vibrant presence lighting up my space, and she stayed until Monday when we went back to work together. It baffled me that she wasn't swarmed with admirers; she revealed she'd had three boyfriends who ended up living with her, but none worked out, so she sent them packing. Thanks to her mom, who left her the house, she was fiercely independent.

If Elena did end things for good, I'd definitely see more

of Susie. I really like her. Of course, that would depend on Susie wanting to see me more.

Her dark, long hair framed her stunning face, and her black eyes sparkled with mischief.

"I'm going to miss this time at your place—like, really miss it," Susie said, tracing patterns on the kitchen counter with her fingertip, her voice tinged with sadness.

"Why's that?" I asked, scrubbing the bowl we used for the cookies.

"Elena's coming back soon. She didn't give me a date, but it sounds imminent," she replied, her gaze darting toward the window as if expecting Elena.

Pages of Passion Book 4: Threads of Destiny

"Even when she's here, we'd love having you around," I reassured her, the scent of freshly baked cookies wrapping us in warmth.

"Thanks, Jefe," she giggled, her cheeks flushing. "Oops, I meant G."

"With you here, I manage to forget about Elena, even though I care about her a lot," I admitted, my voice softening.

"She's lucky to have you," Susie said.

"No, I'm the lucky one," I corrected her, still feeling the sting that Elena had dropped the news of her Hawaii trip with an ex-fling so abruptly. Though we had agreed to see other people, I couldn't help but feel a bit resentful. Did I want Elena back? Yes.

"Alexa's been asking why you don't invite her over," Susie said, changing the subject. She grabbed a cookie and took a bite, the music from the hi-fi filling the small apartment.

"I had no idea she wanted to come," I replied, surprised.

"Jefe, she brings it up every day!" Susie rolled her eyes playfully.

"Funny you mention that. When Elena said she was leaving, she made a point to tell me that I had you and Alexa to hang out with. I wonder why she thought of Alexa?" I mused, leaning back in my chair.

"You just don't see it. Alexa stares at you every chance she gets!" Susie exclaimed, her eyes wide as if revealing a grand secret. "Even Elena knows."

"I've nosed around with Mike and asked him if he's done it with her, and he doesn't deny it."

"Mike is a hunk. Sure, they've been together."

You don't have to answer," I said. Before I said anything else, Susie said, "he's never gotten into my panties. Nope."

"As hot as you are, come on."

"Nope. He hasn't even tried."

It was none of my business to ask her if she'd do it if he approached her.

George Hatcher

* * *

Elena returned just like she'd left, with very little warning. She arrived at the shop in a taxi at about noon on a Monday.

Susie and Alexa didn't have customers, so they ran out to help her with two suitcases. I was sure she had only left with one.

I was in my office by a window that commanded a view of the entire shop, the Brooklyn Avenue entrance, the parking lot, and the Rowan Avenue entrance. I could have run down the stairs to greet her, but I stayed by the window watching her arrival.

Elena opened the trunk of my car then helped Susie and Alexa with the suitcases. As the girls walked in, Elena looked up at the office and saw me.

I smiled.

She smiled.

She double-timed it up the stairs and was in my arms for five minutes of kisses, hugs, and exploring hands. She sat at my desk to take off her heels and put on her flats, which gave her a bird's eye view of my desktop record of check cashing outlets.

Elena made the sign of the cross.

"Baby, how much are you in the hole?"

George Hatcher

"It's under control," I said.

It was under control. As long as I kept cashing checks and making deposits, not a single check ever bounced; it was under control. If a check ever bounced, my credibility would go down the toilet in a heartbeat. If Holmberg or Kitty ever bounced a check of mine, it would be a day of reckoning. I knew nothing lasts forever.

Elena was jet-lagged. As much as I wanted to go, it was too early for me to leave, so I had Susie drive her home in my car. I was on the shop floor most of the time. I put my heart and soul into selling, but I was careful not to push. With the right well-placed suggestion, a person who came in just to paint their car would decide that it was worth the extra twenty to take out the small dent on the fender. I sold a lot of upholstery repairs and jobs for Paulo and his brother. If I wasn't in my office grabbing a quickie with Elena, my spare time was spent with Jose or Paulo. Even though I had the painting down to a science, I still monitored the preparation of the cars and the length of time a car remained in the oven. Not all cars are the same. Of course, Luis was the real expert. He's the one who taught me what I knew, just as the bodyman taught me about dents, Bondo, grinders, and sanding.

After closing up, I went home and found Elena in the pool. She was all smiles and as tan as you'd expect anyone to be who had spent three weeks in Hawaii. The new white bikini she wore showed off her tan.

"Join me, baby."

I went in to change and got in the pool. It was a Monday afternoon, and we were the only ones in the water.

Ava and Emma waved from their apartment window. Elena waved back. We'd had three heated nights. Three times while Elena had been gone.

"How's the jet lag? I thought you were coming home to nap," I said, climbing down the pool stairs. It was a hot day, but the water felt chilly. I gave her a light kiss.

"I slept over two hours; feel good."

I kissed her again and saw my two friends were no longer at the window.

We showered together. No sex was involved, but it was still nice.

We changed into loungewear and started talking about dinner.

As if I'd known she was on her way back, I had stocked up on cheese, crackers, and the odd things I seldom shopped for but that Elena liked.

"I'll fix us a platter," she said. "I don't want dinner, dinner."

"I'll help you."

"Get us some wine, baby."

We sat on the sofa like we did at the office, with the platter between us, our wine on the coffee table an arm's reach away. The platter was organized as only Elena did: pepper-stuffed green olives, crackers, cheese, dried apricots, walnuts, pecans, and strawberry jelly, which I liked when I spooned peanut butter.

I offered a toast.

"Welcome home."

"Thank you, baby."

We drank.

"Best thing I did was to switch to wine," I said. "I've been so good you would not believe it."

She fed me a piece of cheese.

"You were busy fucking the nights away since I've been gone."

She had been gone three weeks. "I'll tell you if you tell me," I said.

"I missed you so much," she said.

"What else did you miss?"

"I missed my car. I love my little convertible."

I felt like reminding her of the Rolls Convertible she'd told me the Texan was driving when they met. I didn't mention

Elena and I worked from open to close and went home together.

"I didn't take a good look last night. You bought new wine. Very nice. You've become a wine buyer."

I opened a bottle of red. For me, red was it.

I poured a nip. We both emptied our glasses so fast it was funny.

"You know what I feel like doing?"

it. She said nothing about her Hawaii trip. She didn't ask me what I did while she was gone either, so I volunteered nothing.

We went to bed that night, hugging and kissing as we always did, but something was different that first night. There was no sex. And I was fine with that.

In the morning, I was up and ready to jog. She was running about two minutes late, getting on her running gear.

"Baby, the trip had to beat you up. You don't have to jog or go to work. Take it easy. It's okay."

She ignored me. "Baby, come on. Let's hit it."

I felt like asking her if she jogged in Hawaii would be stupid, but why had she been gone three weeks?

Fifteen minutes after we started jogging, we hit the base of what she called the mountain. We exchanged looks and began the climb. She kept up with me, just as she did before she left for Hawaii. Three weeks away had not slowed her down.

We were facing each other, and she stretched her right leg on the sofa and her left across my lap.

"We went to sleep last night without it," she said. licking her lips or maybe licking the wine from her lips. "Is that what you want to do now?"

"What I was thinking is that we should head out to the west side or Hollywood. When I was just a punky kid, I was going to nightclubs. Now that I'm old enough, I sit here in my apartment like a hermit."

"Hey, I'm here with you, and I'm no hermit."

"No wonder you sprang to Hawaii. You were bored to death."

"Wrong, baby. I didn't spring because I was bored."

"Let's go eat a great steak, and I don't mean Steven's Steakhouse."

"Where?"

"Santa Monica and I don't mean to the pier like we do. I've seen a lot of restaurants along the street above the bluff."

"You want to do that?"

"I do. I just need a clean shirt. You already look great."

I put on a clean T-shirt and a button-down over it.

"I'll be ready in ten. No shower. I'm going as is."

She went into the extra bedroom where most of her clothes were and emerged in a short skirt and a dressy V-neck.

"You look fuckin fantastic in a skirt," I said.

She grinned at me, and we walked through the garage toward our cars.

"Baby, I'll drive," she said as we approached the car. "I'm not drinking."

Before I answered, she was already in the car, and the top was being lowered.

"I'm not drinking either," I said, sitting in the passenger side.

She leaned just enough to get a good angle on my lips. A good kiss.

A really good kiss. I don't know how long we were at it.

"We can stay home," she said.

Before I answered, the top of the Mustang was already closing.

"We can go out tomorrow. I want to go down on you. I want you to go down on me. I want to hug you all night and pretend I never left."

I unlocked the door to my apartment. She walked up the stairs, me behind her, her skirt hiked up, my hand latching onto her panties.

"Rip them off," she said.

I complied. In bed, I was on top, her legs over my shoulders. We both liked that position.

On a warm Sunday afternoon, Elena invited Susie over, and I gladly covered the taxi fare, eager for some much-needed company. The moment Susie arrived, the atmosphere shifted—her vibrant energy spread like a warm glow throughout the room. Snacks of all kinds were expertly laid out on the coffee table, enticing aromas wafting from chocolate-covered treats and buttery popcorn, filling the air with sweet and salty notes.

Elena casually mentioned that we were out of coffee, and without missing a beat, Susie jumped up, her enthusiasm palpable. She grabbed my car keys and dashed out the door, her laughter trailing behind her as she promised to return quickly with our favorite brew. It was her way of caring—always attentive to our whims, making it effortless to unwind.

Once she left, Elena and I sprawled on the bed, our bodies sinking into the soft, inviting mattress. We rolled face-to-face, the fabric of the sheets cool against our skin, and I could feel a spark of connection. "I love that, Susie," I said, recalling the joking moment when Elena had claimed if she were a man, she would have pursued Susie. "I remember when you said if you were a man, you'd fuck her."

"Yeah, I did," Elena replied with a sly smile. "I said that the day you hired her."

"She was great company," I continued, my voice softer, tinged with a hint of longing. "It's lonely here without you."

Elena raised an eyebrow, teasing me. "How about the working girls?" she asked, referring to Ava and Emma.

"They were both over. It was savage," I admitted, a wry smile crossing my lips.

Elena burst into laughter, the sound ringing like music in the air. "Savage? Where did that come from?"

I paused, contemplating whether I should share the source of my spontaneity. But as the moment slipped away, I kept my thoughts to myself.

Later, her curiosity about Susie resurfaced. "Was she over every night?"

"No," I said, shaking my head gently. "What about you and the Texan? Did you do it every day and night?"

Elena chuckled lightly. "Baby, he's old enough to be my grandfather. Nothing savage there."

Just then, Susie re-entered the room, her arms laden with coffee and a hint of mischief in her eyes. "You told me to take care of him, and I did," she chimed in, the ambient sounds of the soft music and the muted TV setting a relaxed backdrop for our banter.

Elena turned to Susie, a warm smile spreading across her face as she leaned in, kissing her lightly on the lips. We lay back against the plush pillows, fully clothed, as the world outside faded away. The room felt like a cocoon—a blend of comfort, laughter, and subtle tension, where friendship and playful secrets danced in the air like the notes of the trendy tunes floating around us.

Later, I drove Elena and Susie to the Brown Derby on Wilshire Boulevard near the Miracle Mile. It was a fancy place but not stuffy, and we were greeted with warm smiles as we settled in. Virgin margaritas arrived, served by the pitcher, their tangy sweetness mixing with the salty-rimmed glasses we clinked together, pretending we were toasting with something stronger. I opted for the porterhouse steak, perfectly cooked and weighing in at over two pounds, while the girls chose more modest cuts. As I savored each bite, I couldn't help but think of Donna eating a salad the last time I indulged in a huge steak at the Flamingo. Why was I dining with two beautiful women and yet thinking about a third? Decades later, I'd come to realize it was the stress of my business problems weighing me down. In my early twenties, my testosterone levels were probably off the chart, leaving me caught in a whirlwind of desires and distractions.

We didn't get back to my apartment until one in the morning. I was so full I wanted to jog immediately, but Elena and Susie convinced me not to leave when they were so willing. As it turned out, we rolled around the bed, hugging and kissing and talking nonsense until we finally fell asleep.

George Hatcher

* * *

In the morning, it was just Elena and me on the jog. As we frequently did, we talked shop until we got to the mountain.

"Baby, how do you plan to cover the checks you have out? I saw three new check cashing places on your planner."

"You been snooping?"

"How could I miss it? The writing pad takes up half the desk."

I laughed and kissed her as I did, not an easy thing to do at a jog.

"I'd like to know how I got so buried." But I knew.

"Don't chance another trip to Vegas."

"I went to Vegas once while you were gone. It didn't last an hour."

She didn't ask how much I lost.

"Baby, don't go back. I love you," she said as we turned the corner, the steep street, the challenge.

"I love you, too," I said.

We exchanged smiles, then fell into a comfortable silence. The uphill jog was challenging, drawing our attention inward and sharpening our focus.

* * *

When we got to the shop, I let the girls handle the morning customers. I went up to my office. I called Mike at his shop.

"If I could only find another place like this one," I said. "I'd have two cows."

"This Whittier shop is a cow," Mike said.

"The only reason you're busy is insurance. I don't know what's wrong with the people that cruise by you."

"You have Safeway across the street from you, That huge building with all that parking."

"You have a theatre across the street from you," I said.

"People don't come to the show until night unless it's weekend, and we're closed on Sundays."

"Your cash flow sucks," I said.

"I'll start wearing long-sleeved shirts. Maybe my biceps have something to do with no one stopping."

"You are so full of yourself," I said, laughing.

"We're doing okay. Don't knock it, G."

"We're doing good only because Sam buys the paper at the end of the month. What happens if he says no more?"

"I'll go out and cash checks, pay the bills, and cash more checks to cover the checks I wrote."

"You're as crazy as me," I said. I was still laughing when I hung up.

I was a ballsy, stupid kid, bulletproof. I wasn't afraid. After all, I did the locker thing weeks after doing time. That says it all.

***

I went to talk with Chester. He was already holding eight thousand, four checks for two thousand each. "I'm in a bind, but I don't want to get you in trouble."

"Talk to me," he said.

"I need to hit Vegas again. I'm buried nearly a hundred."

I wrote one check for ten thousand from my personal account at Kitty's bank. Chester knew I didn't have the money in the account. He agreed to hold it.

"Are we good?"

Chester said, "We're good."

I put two hundred in the tray under the bullet-proof glass.

He tossed cash on the tray and sent it back to me.

"Give it to me if you come back a winner."

We exchanged smiles. Chester knew about my Vegas wins.

He punched the two-inch glass between us, and I punched from outside. I stuffed the money in my pockets. Bullet-proof high fives.

I headed straight for Vegas without stopping at the shop.

About an hour and a half from Vegas, I stopped to gas up in Baker. I'd be shocked if there were more than two pay phones in that sliver of a town. I made a collect call to the shop. Susie answered and accepted the call.

"Are you in jail or something?"

I laughed. "Not yet. Give me a little time."

"I'll get her," she said.

Elena picked up.

"Baby, tell me you're not in Vegas."

"I'm not in Vegas," I said. "I'm in Baker. Got another hour and change to go."

Elena sighed. "Good luck, baby. No matter what, I'm with you."

Chapter 7

Las Vegas

When I made it to Vegas, I drove past the Tropicana to the Dunes Hotel. It was a fucking fantastic place, a resort like I'd never seen before. I wished I was there on vacation with Elena, but I was in the opposite situation. I knew no one. I had nothing coming. No one knew me. Once again, I had left on the fly, and the clothes I had on were all I had. Fuck the rules about resting after arrival.

Fuck it.

It was just getting dark outside, but I couldn't tell inside the casino. I wondered how old the place was. It looked new. When I arrived, I parked myself, bundled up the cash I had into one-thousand-dollar bundles, folded it, and stashed it in my two front pockets. I put the five hundred dollars of walking around money in a back pocket. In the front was a giant sultan with his hands on his hips. When you went in the front, you entered right below where he was standing on the roof. Inside rooms had Arabian nights-styled names.

The Dunes was not packed like the Tropicana and the Fremont. Maybe it was early for the crowds. I looked for a table with action, but every table had two players at the most. Fuck.

I took the extreme.

I found a pretty brunette named Jane just standing there, ready for a player to sit down. The name tag didn't say where she was from. I sat down at her table. All the casinos hired lookers to be dealers, and Jane just proved that rule. The long-sleeved white shirts and ties dealers wore here looked really classy on her.

I like a table with a lady dealer.

"Hi Jane," I said and took the seat to her left. I was solo at the table. I had never played that way before. If Mike had been there, he would have had a baby in disgust.

I reached into my pocket and put a thousand on the table. "Money plays, Jane."

She counted and said, "Money plays."

The pit boss appeared from out of nowhere. "Money plays." He smiled at me and walked away as they do.

She had a blackjack, and I had a blackjack.

"Good start, Jane."

I patted the cash on the table to indicate I was playing one thousand.

I had a high card showing and another buried. Dealer had a deuce showing. She drew a seven and stayed. I was paid in hundred-dollar chips.

"Money plays, plus a thousand in chips."

Jane didn't count the thousand that had been on the table, but she did call it.

"Money plays."

"Money plays," the pit boss repeated from afar.

I got a blackjack.

I tossed a hundred-dollar chip to Jane. She clicked the chip on the table, smiled, and put it in her shirt pocket.

I put my thousand cash back in my pocket and started playing with chips. Thirty minutes later, I changed color from hundreds to thousands. I had fifteen thousand, and I hadn't touched the money in my pocket.

I took a real good look at Jane as she shuffled. She smiled at me like there wasn't a care in the world. I don't think the dealer's care. It's all luck, no funny business. I pushed ten-thousand-dollar chips to play.

Jane busted.

I was as calm as could be when I ordered a glass of ice water. Two people sat down at the table. When I looked back, there were spectators. More people were in the casino now, and some of them were standing around this table. When I had forty thousand in chips, Jane was replaced. I had given her four hundred in tips.

"I'll be back," she said.

A guy named Tom took over. I played a thousand-dollar chip. I didn't notice how much the two people at the table were playing. I looked at Tom. He looked bored. Maybe he was a relief guy. Maybe he was anxious to finish his shift and go home. I had a good feel.

I won the thousand-dollar hand.

I played ten thousand in chips.

I felt a tap on my shoulder, heard a whisper in my ear.

"My name is Lana. Here's my card. Have me paged when you take a break."

I turned around and saw the hot lady. She was probably five years older than me.

"Thanks," I said.

The dealer was waiting for me to check my cards. I did. I had a blackjack.

I didn't want this to be a dream. It was too good. Too good.

When Jane returned, I had given Tom two hundred in tips. In front of me, I had five ten-thousand-dollar chips and about thirty-one-thousand-dollar chips. It was time to split, but I couldn't do it. The table was now full. More cards to go around, more shuffles.

"Hi, Jane," I said.

"How did Tom treat everybody?"

There were mumbles. Jane didn't care.

Everyone had a bet out except me. "Are you in?" she asked me.

"I'll pass this one," I said.

Good thing I did, dealer got blackjack.

Jane smiled at the table, but she gave me a fast look.

I pushed a ten-thousand-dollar chip forward as my play.

I had never played a high chip like that. I had bet more than ten in one hand but not with a ten-thousand-dollar chip.

Jane called out, "Ten thousand dollars plays."

The pit boss walked over to repeat ten-thousand-dollar plays."

I should have been sweating, but I wasn't. I looked around my table because all the players were looking at me. I smiled. I got smiles back and one thumbs up. I didn't turn around, but I could hear there was a group of people behind me. Looking back, I was young and looked it; everyone was much older than me, not just at the Dunes, but at every casino I had ever played. I wonder what people thought of me as I played. In those days, most people dressed up. I wore jeans and a T-shirt.

I won that hand, gave Jane one hundred, and asked her to change my thousand-dollar chips to ten-thousand-dollar chips. I nodded salutations to everyone at the table.

"I'm tired, or I'd stay longer," I said, as though anyone cared.

I got taps on my back and shoulder from people behind me as I worked my way through them away from the table. Once up and ready to walk away, I lifted my glass of water to Jane.

"Thank you, Jane."

"Have a wonderful night," Jane said with a pretty smile.

I went to the cashier with nine ten-thousand-dollar chips. Fuck. So much money. The buying power today would be ten times more than that. I don't know where all the money went that I won back then.

I approached the cashier, a lady who was about fifty years old. She frowned at my ten-thousand-dollar chips.

"Hon make five or six trips with these," she said. "All at once, I have to ask you for a social security number."

I knew what she meant about taxes. It had never happened to me before, and I'd cashed a lot of money before at the Tropicana and Fremont. I'd never cashed in ten thousand in chips. Maybe that's the trigger. I read her name tag.

"Jan, I appreciate it. Can you handle twenty?" She nodded. She took two chips and gave me back seven chips that I put in my pocket.

I gave Jan two hundred. "Thank you," I said. "I'm learning."

She took the tip and put it to the side.

"You can give me another two chips," she said.

Before I left the cashier, I had cashed all the chips, but not all at once. Jan got a total of four hundred dollars.

"If I wasn't behind this cage, I'd hug and kiss you," she said.

I palmed my right hand, kissed it, and reached in for her hand.

"Thank you, Jan."

I wasn't a minute away from the cashier when I saw Lana. I don't think it was a coincidence. I think she was tracking me.

We shook hands. I gave her my Eastland Auto Center card.

"First time with us?"

"Yes," I said. "I normally play at Tropicana or Fremont."

She looked at my card.

"George, we want you here. Our suites are much nicer, and our service is the best."

"I believe you," I said.

"Let me fix you up tonight?"

I dug into my overstuffed pockets and pulled out a hundred-dollar bill. This tip wasn't just for the services of the night; it was an investment in the future. Years later, I found myself surrounded by friends from Vegas who had climbed the ranks to become a pit boss and even a casino boss. The tips I had given them forged our bond; I truly believe that. Yet now, as I look back, I realize that many of those friends are either retired or gone.

I got the most fabulous suite I had ever imagined. I sat in that room and looked out the window, feeling guilty that Elena was not with me. I could see the Flamingo at a distance across many empty lots. The strip was not then what it is now. Next door, the construction of Caesars Palace was just beginning.

I called my apartment.

Elena answered.

"Baby, I'm at the Dunes Hotel. And fuck, I won."

Elena went bananas.

Hearing her, I went bananas, too, alone in my big suite.

"How much did you win?" she asked.

"Ninety thousand," I said.

She squealed, breaking my eardrum.

How much did you win?" she asked again, her voice quivering.

"Ninety thousand," I said.

She squealed again, breaking my eardrum.

She asked me to confirm how much I won three times, and each time I told her, she went crazy.

"You have to be the luckiest person in the world."

"I am. I have you," I said.

"Baby, that's so sweet. I wish you were here."

"I'm too tired," I said. "Seems like a waste that I have this enormous suite, and I'm just going to bed."

"Baby, I'm not telling you what to do, but before you hit another table on this trip, think about it really good."

"I'm not stopping at another table this trip," I said with finality. "I never go more than one day."

I was surprised that Elena didn't ask me if I was going to see the girl I know in Vegas. Donna.

My watch said it was ten after eleven. It felt much later. Here I was again with no change of clothes. It was too late to go out and buy anything. Fuck.

I had Donna's phone number in my wallet. I called. It was a hotel. I asked for her. I was connected to her room, and it rang and rang. The operator asked if I wanted to leave a message.

I left my name.

I put my money in the room safe. Back then, they didn't have digital, only a key. A crooked housekeeper could make out if they got in my safe, but that wasn't going to happen. I left my room and put the do not disturb sign on my double door entry.

Vegas was already a taxi town. I left my car in the lot and took a cab from the front entrance. There had to be twenty cabs lined up, waiting for fares. The cab dropped me off at the Tropicana. It was a seven-minute drive, during which the driver hustled me a little, offered to take me to hangouts that never slept, and to the best cat houses (not yet legal in Nevada.) The oldest profession lived before then and now.

I gave the cabbie a five, and he was delighted. The meter read one dollar twenty cents.

I figured if Donna was not at her hotel, she must be at work. If she was at the bar where I was headed, then she was not doing too good. I walked in-no Donna. I thought of asking for her, but how stupid would that have been?

I was at the bar. All around me, people were drinking. I thought of having one myself. Just one drink wouldn't hurt. But why start? I'd gone all night with no alcohol. I was probably the only person at the Dunes Casino who had been drinking water while gambling.

The feel of the Tropicana was good. The Dunes was great. The Dunes had done me justice that night, but the Tropicana had done me justice a number of times before.

Not the last visit, though. I headed to the entrance to get a cab. On my way, there was Donna walking in as I was going out. Just as I saw her, she saw me. She stopped.

I had just passed through the exit. I walked backwards back into the hotel. She walked up to me. We hugged like we were longtime friends. I'd say we were friends.

"You look beautiful," I said. She still had that Marilyn Monroe look.

"What a surprise," she said. "I got a message that George called, but no phone. I figured it was you and that you were here. And here you are."

I loved the blonde hair, and her brown eyes, and that tiny space between her front teeth.

"I'm at the Dunes," I said. "You got anything going?"

She shook her head, but there was something wrong.

People were walking around us. We blocked the flow of traffic but only paid attention to each other.

"What's wrong?"

"That time of the month."

"Let's keep each other company," I said.

I didn't have to hail a taxi. Plenty of them were waiting. We commandeered one and headed to the Dunes. I put my arm around her like she was my girlfriend.

"I almost called you to see if you'd come to LA and spend a weekend with me."

"I would. Sure."

"Good to know," I said.

She kissed me. I tasted mint. I think it was mint gum that she was no longer chewing.

"Have you been to the Dunes?"

"Yeah," she said. "Fussy. I don't hang around in the bar like at the Tropicana. I get guys who are staying there. That's when I come over."

When she saw the suite, she said it was dazzling.

"Out of this world," she said.

I don't know how Arabian everything was, but it was decorated and spacious.

"Are you hungry?" I asked.

"Not at all, but you eat if you are."

"I'm good," I lied. "Let's see if they have any wine you like."

She brightened. "Yeah."

How could I have been so deeply attached to Elena and still chosen to go out that night to pursue Donna? My agreement with Elena allows for this; it's just a part of the guy experience. It's not always about sex. We spent most of the evening talking, and for once, I found myself listening more than speaking.

* * *

In the morning, I gave Donna a thousand dollars.

To say she was surprised would be an understatement.

"I'll make it right for you," she said, surprised at the ten hundred dollar bills I gave her.

"Your companionship made it right," I said.

"You didn't even let me take care of you," she said.

"I wanted to see you, and I did. I didn't want to be alone last night, and I wasn't. We're good."

We hugged. We kissed. "You're very special, George."

"So are you."

Chapter 8
Putting Out Fires

A little after eleven in the morning, I arrived at the shop. Alexa was with a customer. Susie was driving a car inside to be worked on. I didn't see Elena. I went directly up to the office.

I saw her behind my desk working on deposits. She looked up when I walked in, and I swear her face got brighter when she saw me.

"I have to keep a trip bag in the car," were the first words out of my mouth.

"Baby," she said.

"I'm home," I said.

We came together, so many kisses.

"You won. I could hardly sleep I was so excited for you."

"I didn't get much sleep either."

She tugged my hair, kissed me, and spoke at the same time. It's not always easy to understand what someone is saying when they've got a mouthful of your lower lip. "You showered before you left Vegas to kill the sex smell."

"No way," I said. "No sex."

It was true. There had been zero sex with Donna.

"I believe you, baby."

Under the window, I noticed a café table and a couple of chairs. I walked over and sat on one of the chairs for a second.

"Good deal," I said. "Hey, it matches the desk. We've been needing these for so long. I like. Thanks."

Elena nodded. "We keep talking about a table and chairs. Finally, I went out and found this set. I'm glad you like it."

I got up, walked to the desk, and emptied one pocket.

"I was going to put the money in a bag, but the only bags in the room are shopping bags."

I started pulling out hundred-dollar bills.

"Let's put the money in the safe, head home, and rest for what's left of the day," Elena said. "What do you say?"

"Sit across from me, and let's sort the cash. I'd love to go home early. If we finish, we're out of here. I can't let another day go by without covering the mess of checks I have everywhere."

Elena sat across from me, and we worked the cash.

"Instead of making a huge cash deposit like before, I'm going to only deposit the cash for the checks I know are on their way to the bank. The rest are at the check stores. I want to drive out to them, take my checks back, and give them cash."

"Fantastic," Elena said.

"I owe Chester ten thousand. He's holding a personal check of mine for ten, and he has four two thousand checks for a total of eight thousand that he's been holding."

"Okay, let me separate eighteen thousand for Chester."

"I only touched the ten one time. My seed money was one thousand dollars. From then on, I held my own."

"Fuckin amazing."

Susie came on the intercom.

"Lunch time."

Elena picked up. "Order something, and we'll pay. No lunch today."

"You want something for yourself?"

I shook my head. My stomach wasn't going to be happy till all those checks were taken care of.

"G and I are good," she said and hung up.

"Last night, when I called, I didn't ask if Susie went home with you."

"No, I was alone."

Elena had envelopes out and was writing the names of each place on each envelope. I worked my notes on my desk pad. We bundled up the cash owed at each check-cashing place.

"Here's the bottom line. I need to deposit thirty-one thousand today. That will handle all the checks flying towards the bank."

"We need to deliver sixty-five thousand to the check places, including Chester." Elena added.

"What do I have left?"

Elena laughed. "You have four thousand one hundred left. Do you know how amazing it is you have anything left? That you covered everything?"

"I think five hundred of that was my own money before I got the ten from Chester. I had hoped I'd have over ten left. I wanted to take care of everyone like before."

"Baby, this isn't the time. You just made it through hell by the skin of your teeth."

"Easy come, easy go. Come with me," I said.

"Aren't you hungry?"

"I don't remember the last time I ate. Let's eat after we put out the fires. Is that okay?"

"Let's pretend we're firemen."

Elena had her crazy moments.

* * *

It took us three hours to deposit the cash at Holmberg's bank and make the check-cashing rounds.

"The problem is that all these dudes you paid today were so happy to get the cash before the due date that their doors will be open even wider for you to keep coming back."

"I know. It got out of hand. This time, I was worried the balloon would pop."

We hadn't gone home after giving away the lion's share of the money. We went to Jesse at the meat market to get steaks, and then his chef-prepared them for us. That's a man who knows how to cook meat. We even got baked potatoes.

Elena carried our food on a tray up the stairs to my office. I followed. It was our first meal on the new table. The chairs were two captain chairs like those in the waiting room downstairs, but these were new.

She must have been as hungry as I was and, in record time, did an amazing job polishing off every morsel of her steak and half of her potato.

It was amazing not to have to rough it on the sofa.

Carving steaks was a breeze on an actual table, not to mention Jesse's excellent steak knives.

"I need to go home, shower, and change of clothes."

"First, we do it," she said. "Let's bail!"

"Deal."

Chapter 9
The Looming Abyss

Looking back, the path to the precipice was paved with good intentions and unchecked ambition. If only I had possessed the discipline to shut down those thriving shops on the very day I returned a winner, my bank accounts would have sung a different tune. Not a nickel would have been owed to Chester, Rene, or any of the other three check-cashing operations that had become my lifeline. Sam's agreement to buy a month's worth of receivables for my shop would have, in theory, covered the monthly bills, assuming Mike's Whittier Auto Center broke even upon liquidation. But "if only" is a dangerous game to play with hindsight.

I didn't close the shops. Instead, I let the overhead costs swell like an unchecked tide. In my relentless drive to bring ideas to life, I was blind to critical information, deaf to vital advice. I lacked administrative skills, true business expansion knowledge. Elena's caution about rapid growth echoed her mother's conservative approach to opening a second mortuary; a warning I dismissed, only to see its stark wisdom materialize before my very eyes.

Donald, ever the blunt instrument of truth, offered his unvarnished opinion. "George, you need to raise your prices. Or, more simply, shut down the shops that aren't making money."

I bristled, the words tasting like ash. "So, before it was the insurance work. Now you say the prices are too low?"

"George, it's both. Soto isn't breaking even. Neither is the Car Wash Shop. Every month, they're costing you money just to keep their doors open."

The truth landed with the dull thud of a heavy weight. He was right, and I hated him for it.

That morning, I met Sam for breakfast in his usual booth at Canter's Deli. Eunice, her black hair a towering bun atop her head, new cat's-eye glasses perched on her nose, navigated the crowded tables with a fresh pot of coffee in hand, secrets undoubtedly tucked into the massive pockets of her waitress uniform. A massive breakfast plate for Sam; a Denver omelet for me, though my appetite was already dwindling.

"Georgie," Sam began, his voice surprisingly gentle for the news he was about to deliver. "I've set aside a hundred thousand to buy receivables from you and Mike.

It's like a credit line. You send me checks when money comes in from insurance. I turn around and buy more receivables as you need. But if a month-end comes, and I'm out a hundred, I can't buy anything more until I see some collections."

A ceiling. A hard limit. My stomach dropped. "Got it, Sam. I appreciate all you do for me." The words felt hollow.

Sam gave me a knowing look. "It's a two-way street, Georgie. I appreciate the business you give me." But I heard the unspoken condition: *keep the business good, or this lifeline disappears.*

That afternoon, Mike's shop seemed a whirlwind of activity, a comforting illusion of prosperity. Yet, I knew how much of that bustle was tied up in slow-paying insurance work. I laid out Sam's new terms. "You can't count on selling everything you're owed like before, Mike. Not unless the total balance due to Sam is less than a hundred thousand. He has a ceiling now."

Mike's grin didn't falter, but a flicker of concern crossed his eyes. "I'll call the adjusters. Get them to send checks faster."

I knew that trick. It worked for a short while, a temporary reprieve, but it wasn't a solution. Still, I didn't want to be too discouraging. "Good idea," I said, forcing a cheerful tone. "Stay on it. Remember, it's not just you using up that hundred from Sam. I'm selling my paper to him, too."

"I got it," Mike said, extending his hand. We shook, and he pulled me into a quick, firm hug before I left. I returned it, a silent plea for strength.

Downstairs, back in my own shop, a lull settled between the morning intake and the evening pick-up rush. I found Elena and recounted my grim breakfast with Sam. "He may be doing me a favor," I mused, more to myself than to her. "But if we can't sell him all the paper, we're not paying the juice. And it's big juice."

Elena kissed me, her touch a small comfort. "Oh baby, but you need the cash flow." She was right. The cash flow was everything, a river I was desperate to keep from drying up. My biggest win from Vegas, the one that bought us precious time, had evaporated in hours upon my return.

"Maybe we can cut overhead somewhere," I suggested, knowing it was a futile gesture.

"Baby, you have Luis making two hundred fifty dollars a week. He used to be happy with a hundred." Her voice was gentle, but her words were razor sharp.

"Luis was my inspiration, my first employee. Without him, I'd be out to lunch fast. Are you saying I should cut his pay?" The thought was unbearable.

"No, you can't do that," she conceded, then pressed on. "But you have too many employees, George, and all of them are making more than they ever made anywhere else. It adds up."

"It's the way I run my business," I retorted, my voice tight. My pride was on the line, but deep down, I knew she was right.

"It may not be all of the problem, but you have a killer payroll. Donald brings it up every month. The upholsterers were supposed to get a draw only at the start. Now they get a draw if business slows down."

I sighed, a sound that carried the weight of my crumbling empire. The walls were closing in, the numbers refusing to bend to my will. "I feel like a beer. I'm going next door." I pushed away from the table, leaving my untouched lunch. I was still full from Sam's omelet, or perhaps just from the bitter taste of impending doom. If Elena said anything as I walked out, I didn't hear it. The clinking of beer bottles next door called to me, promising a brief, false escape from the harsh arithmetic of reality.

Chapter 10
The Latin Playboy Bar

There was a beer bar across the street from the shop. It took two minutes to cross the street and get there. It was called the Latin Playboy; imagine that one. They had a jukebox with a decent selection, and I liked the ambiance. I thought of the jukebox I had in my first business, an ice cream parlor in Juarez, Mexico.

I had started going there when Elena was in Hawaii. They had good sandwiches, beer, and wine. Not great wine. None of the better wines I'd been getting used to. They also served beer in a frosty mug. Adrian, a hot brunette about my height, worked behind the counter from lunchtime until eight at night. Her hair was long and curly, and her dresses were usually cut in a deep V, showing off generous cleavage. I'd never been there at night. The light was dimmer than outside, and it took a few seconds for me to be able to see well. When I did, it was strange to me that it was so empty. I didn't know when their crowds arrived, but halfway between lunch and dinner, I guess, was not it.

"Hey, stranger," Adrian said as I walked in.

"Hey back," I said, taking a seat at the bar. "Where is everyone?"

"Too early." She poured me a beer and placed it in front of me. "Extra cold like you like."

"I think I'll have a hamburger," I said.

"Well done. No tomatoes. No lettuce."

"You have a great memory."

She wrote my order in her ticket book, disappeared down

a hall, and came right back. I knew she'd placed the order back in the kitchen.

"You don't come over much," she said.

"It's crazy busy. I get food at the meat market and eat at the shop."

"Yeah, that's what you said before."

I smiled. "Same story, sorry."

Adrian laughed. She had a nice laugh.

"Starting next week, my hours will change. I open at noon like now, but I leave at four."

"Only four hours?"

"No, I'll be working a split shift. I leave at four. James's wife will work from four until eight. I come back at eight and work to close at midnight. Just so you know."

I met the owner, James. He was a young, friendly guy. I did a small bodywork repair on his Chevrolet and spot-painted it to match the original.

"Is his wife as pretty as you?"

It wasn't the first time she leaned over the bar and got right up to my face. She chewed gum, but she chewed it sexy.

"Her name is Molly. If I say so myself, she's beautiful. Do me a favor. Come by. Maybe you can steal her away from her husband so that I get James."

"Oh, I see. You like James?"

"I adore James."

I sipped my beer.

"Adrian, when you get serious, you're even prettier."

"Keep saying things like that, and I might fall in love with you, too."

"You don't want to do that," I said.

I heard a bell ring, and Adrian went to pick up my food.

The hamburger was decent. Condiments were in reach: ketchup, mayo, mustard, pickles, peppers, hot sauce. I added mustard and pickles and started eating away.

"Be sure you come back when she's working next week," Adrian said, still gossiping with me. Not another customer was in sight.

"Why would James want her to work here?"

"Hey, that's offensive."

"I didn't mean it like that. His place. You'd think he'd be jealous or something."

Adrian laughed. "No big deal. They have a four-year-old daughter."

"Nice," I said.

"He fools around on her. It's not as nice as you might think."

"Does he know you love him? You don't need to answer that."

"He knows. We've been out together. I'm sure Molly knows. When she comes here, she talks to me, but I can tell she knows."

"Maybe she doesn't know."

"She knows."

I finished the burger and half the beer and split.

I was not a beer drinker, but their hamburgers are okay. I liked Adrian, the atmosphere, and the continuous music.

Elena was on the shop floor. She saw me walk in. I walked over and kissed her.

"Baby, beer. Beer during working hours," she frowned, but it switched to a laugh.

"When you were away with the Texan, I found this little tavern next door. I never drink more than half a mug." I wasn't sure why I was explaining.

"You didn't finish your lunch."

"I ate a hamburger with the beer."

A customer drove up in a beater, a fifty-eight Chevrolet coupe with faded paint, a dent in the fender, and a long scratch down the side. Elena gave me an indecipherable look and walked away.

In the mechanic department, Jose had four cars in his four stalls and ran his department with the help of a mechanic and a helper. He now worked for me. No more splits. It saved me from the math. I was paying him a lot more than he could make anywhere else, and he told me so.

Jose was replacing a short block on a Ford. We bought the short blocks, rebuilt by none other than Eagle Parts, Sam. The short block is the part of the engine that has the pistons. The heads are bolted to the short block, and that's where the spark plugs are screwed onto. I don't mean to give you a lesson on mechanics, and there is always a chance that after all these years, I may write something that could be just a little incorrect.

"The gaskets were stuck on the heads of the motor, and I am moistening them with grease so I can peel them off," Jose said.

I totally understood the workings of an engine. Didn't matter what kind of car. Basically, they were the same.

If Sam had a short block in stock for the car Jose was working on, it's fair to say that the car would be ready twenty-four hours after it was dropped off. If Sam didn't have the rebuilt short block- and that was rare—it could take an extra day.

I went up to the office. After a while. Elena came in.

"I'm sorry I walked out on you," I said.

"I feel your stress," she said, leaning toward me.

"You can't feel my stress."

"Want to get rid of it inside of me?"

"Who is gross now?"

Our eyes met. I saw a tiny grin cross her face.

"Don't play hard to get," she said, putting her hands on her hips like she was posing.

I walked over to the new table, freed myself, and sat in one of the captain's chairs. I beckoned her with a finger.

Her jeans dropped to the floor, and she stepped out of them. She took off her panties with lightning speed. She sat, and I went inside with no guidance.

"Slow baby," she said. "Watch how good you're going to feel when we're done."

I hugged her by the waist. Our lips pressed against each other. It was not slow. It was fierce.

Chapter 11
Always Something

It had been months since my big win when Elena told me that Mr. Graham from Bank of America was on the phone. I had always dealt with Mr. Holmberg. I had no idea why this Mr. Graham would be calling, but he didn't let me wonder for long.

"Mr. Hatcher, I'm calling you concerning your Eastland Auto Center account. It is overdrawn."

"I will have it all covered with today's deposit. Where's Mr. Holmberg?"

"On leave," he said curtly. "Mr. Hatcher, have you made deposits today?"

"Not yet. I normally get there before three."

"Mr. Hatcher, if you plan to cover the checks that are causing the overdraft, you'll have to be here before noon. Please see me personally."

I hung up and stared at the phone, wondering about the stranger. Who the fuck was this?

I called back.

"Where is he?" I asked Connie, Holmberg's secretary.

"Oh, George. You don't know, do you?" she said, her voice choking.

"What is it?" Something terrible had happened. The ever-cheerful Connie was crying.

"His wife and son were in an accident last night. They were both killed."

Memories rushed back. I remembered a conversation once about the son I had never met. I always spoke of helping to get him a job. The pictures of him were on the desk in Mr. Holmberg's office.

I ran to the restroom, where I vomited, then cried.

Elena came after me and found me leaning against the wall with my arms braced, forehead pressed against the tile. I felt her cool hand against the back of my neck, heard her voice close to my ear.

"My God G, you're white as a sheet."

Immediately, I sent Elena to the bank with the deposits for Mr. Graham. I went down to the floor to take her place. It was a busy morning and dealing with customers kept me from dwelling on the news about Mr. Holmberg's family. Alexa's voice came on the intercom.

"Mr. Graham on the line for you, George."

The sick feeling came back with a rush. I took the phone upstairs in my office while I was looking out over the shop.

"Mr. Hatcher, I have been anticipating meeting you. I've been looking over your loan file and the records of your checking accounts."

Graham was a prick.

"Excuse me, Mr. Graham. I have always dealt with Mr. Holmberg and plan to continue dealing with him. My loans are current. Yes, my accounts have been overdrawn in the past, but I have always covered them-"

"Mr. Hatcher, until Mr. Holmberg returns, you will have to deal with me. I will not give you the future courtesy of calling when you are overdrawn again. If the money isn't here, checks go back. Bank policy looks down on overdrafts, more so when the customer has a loan relationship with the bank.

I had more to lose than he did. I don't know how, but I managed to sound easier to get along with. "I understand. I'll take a hard look at my checking account balance and get the deposits in before a check goes out."

"Thank you for your understanding," he said. The asshole softened.

The bank was not far from the shop. Elena returned while I was still on the phone with Graham. I saw her walk in.

She headed straight for the stairs and waited for me to hang up.

"I always know exactly what I'm short," I told her. "Before Holmberg offered to cover me when I didn't have enough in the account, I was never overdrawn. I made the deposit before mailing the checks. I need to do that again. This prick will bounce the checks if the money is not there."

"Let me know how I can help," Elena said.

"Thanks. Tomorrow I'll figure out if I am short. If so, I'll get Chester to hold a check and deposit the cash."

I had never met Holmberg's son or wife. The pictures were always proudly in plain view, but I had no memory of what they looked like. I felt haunted by the news. Mr. Holmberg had always had such a paternal relationship with me. I felt like I needed to do something. I picked up the phone.

"Connie, I owe so much to Mr. Holmberg. I would like to do something to show my respect. Is there a service somewhere I could attend?"

"That's very kind of you, George. I will let Mr. Holmberg know you inquired. I believe they are having a private service, just for the family."

"Do you know where I could send flowers?"

Connie gave me the address of the funeral home.

I sent an arrangement of flowers

* * *

"You think he'll be back to work someday?" Elena asked.

"Good question. Nothing lasts forever," I said. "I need to paddle my own canoe without Holmberg's help. I hope he gets through this tragedy."

"Every funeral is a sad event," Elena said.

"I can understand why you didn't stick around the funeral business."

"I never say never. For now, you're right. I'm out of the business."

I was so torn that I didn't bother to ask her what she meant.

* * *

Three days later, Elena said, "Mr. Lewis is on the phone from Atlantic Ford. He says he has a returned check for eighteen hundred dollars."

I took the phone.

"Put it back through, Mr. Lewis. The money is there. The deposit was late. I'm really sorry."

Immediately, I phoned Graham.

"Mr. Graham, I think we might have a personality problem. My businesses can't afford it. If-"

"Mr. Hatcher," he interrupted. "You are wrong. There is no personality problem. I must warn you that if you continue to write checks before you have the money on deposit, I will have no alternative but to close your account."

I was on the verge of blowing it. I tried to keep my cool. "Mr. Graham, I balanced my checkbook and made a cash deposit to cover what I believed were all the checks outstanding. I wish you had called me. I would have run over there with the shortage."

"I told you before, no more courtesy calls. I have my hands full taking over Mr. Holmberg's position. Don't write a check unless the money is in the account. Good afternoon, Mr. Hatcher." He hung up hard. It sounded very final.

I called Connie for feedback.

"Who is this guy? He's nuts!"

"He's a lifer with the bank. Takes him one hour to get here in the morning and longer to get home after closing. He hates this assignment."

I asked her to send my warm regards to Mr. H if she happened to speak with him. She mentioned that she hadn't been invited to the funeral, which I found strange but chose not to say anything about. At that time, my knowledge of funerals was limited to what Elena occasionally shared. Growing up in Douglas, Arizona, my mom and I attended wakes whenever a neighbor or friend passed away; these gatherings typically took place at the family's home. I remember my mom telling her friends that if you could get through the first three months of the year, you'd probably be around for the rest. I suppose she was referring to those who passed away early in the year. She also often remarked that most people didn't live past the age of sixty-five. I never attended a funeral until much later in my life.

Elena was worried that there might be other checks the banker bounced. "

"I don't think so. I thought I had covered everything, but apparently, I should have looked closer at the math."

"Write the checks from Kitty's bank, not from Bank of America."

"The six thousand I got from Chester is to deposit there. I gave Chester two-three thousand checks from that account to hold. I haven't tested Kitty with an overdraft," I said.

"Baby, don't test her. Do like before. Add up the checks and deposit the money before you send them out. If you must, do what you did before. Go cash a check and take the cash to cover what you're short."

I knew that's what I had to do.

I nodded in agreement.

I figured Kitty would have told me if Mike overdrew the Whittier Auto Center account. Or maybe she wouldn't tell me because he was fucking her. I had to call Mike and see.

"How you doing at the bank?"

"What do you mean?"

"Are you ever overdrawn?"

"How could I be overdrawn? You showed me how to cash checks if I had to and deposit the money before the checks hit. I've never been overdrawn."

"Well, I'll be damned," I said. "You the man, Mike."

"Shame on me," I told Elena. "Mike says he's never been overdrawn because I taught him what to do to prevent it."

"You mean the teacher fucked up?"

"Yep. I thought I was good at math. Holmberg should never have said he'd cover me on a daily basis whenever I didn't have enough money. I abused that, and now I have an enemy in Holmberg's chair."

"I don't think he's an enemy. Go see him, smooth it out with him."

"I'm afraid if he gives me a bad time, I'll blow it, and he'll close my account. I'll just chill for now. I'll cover Chester's six thousand and then no more checks from that bank until I'm sure everything has cleared."

"Good move, Baby."

Chapter 12
Being Boss Is A Bitch

I loved being my own boss, but juggling to keep everything afloat was wearing me down. It was depressing. I spent more time at my desk figuring out what checks I needed to cover before they hit the bank than I did on the floor doing actual work. I wasn't in the hole as much as before, but little by little, the balloon grew. Mike gave me six thousand one month for my cut of the business. He did more insurance work than I did because I fixed it with the adjusters to send him more. He had a shop that wasn't painting more than two cars a day, so he had the room and help to do a lot of insurance repairs.

Every check from insurance was deposited, and immediately, I wrote a check to Sam for the full amount so that we'd stay under the hundred thousand he had committed to.

Chapter 13
Molly

Lunching with Elena had become a familiar ritual, making sightings of Adrian at the Playboy tavern for a casual beer and sandwich rare. However, I did make a habit of dropping by post-four in the afternoon for a drink after encountering Molly, the enchanting wife of the bar owner. Adrian's depiction of her was accurate; she was truly stunning, a beautiful blonde. Whether her hair was naturally blonde or dyed was irrelevant; the authenticity of its color seemed immaterial.

All the stools were filled at the bar, and I was convinced it was because Molly was tending the bar. She was totally hot material. When I was there, I nursed the beer, seldom finished it, and always turned down the offer to cap it.

"I don't think you're a beer drinker," Molly said.

"I used to be. I dig the ice-cold mugs and the foam, but you're right. I'm more into wine."

"We have wine," Molly said.

"I know, but I'm just beginning to learn wine. My taste is fussy."

"You can say you don't like the wine here," she said with a big smile.

I laughed. "You're right, Molly."

She was attentive to all the customers. It was hard to carry on a conversation because there were eighteen stools at the bar. I counted them. What little time she gave me was little by little. We chatted. When I didn't get there at five after four, she'd say, "I thought you might not make it today."

She had to know I was mesmerized by her. I think my attention was transparent.

Elena noticed my absence in the late afternoon. It was never a long absence, but she asked why I was frequenting the tavern so much.

"It's like a short break from it all," I said. "I never finish the beer, and I never eat there anymore because it's too close to dinner."

"Good, baby. If you need that little break, go for it."

* * *

The owner of Rene's Check Cashing was a good friend. If I told him I needed to cash a check for eight thousand and wanted him to hold it for a week, he'd figure out his cost. He told me one day that he could front me up to fifteen thousand for up to eight banking days if I needed that much. I didn't take him up on it right away, but eventually, I did.

It was bound to happen. Nothing is perfect, and even when it is, it doesn't last forever. One day, Rene's assistant deposited a check that was supposed to be held for an agreed-upon number of days.

"Mr. Hatcher, you have twenty-five hundred in your account and a check is in for fifteen thousand."

I couldn't tell him that Rene's Check Cashing was supposed to hold the checks until I told him to deposit. No telling what this worm would think or accuse me of.

"Mr. Graham, I'm sorry about the overdraft. If you check, I'm not writing checks from your bank in hopes of getting the account balanced out. Please let me bring a cash deposit, and I promise this is it."

There was silence on his end of the line, and I waited it out somehow.

"You better hurry," Graham said and hung up.

I told Elena, and she said, "I thought you weren't writing checks from that account."

"I wasn't thinking," I said.

I took a blank check from Kitty's bank and drove to Rene's. He was apologetic.

"No reason to be sorry," I said. "Can I get $13,000 from you? Take what you need to hold for a week."

"Is the fifteen going to clear?"

"Rene, of course. I will never let you down."

"G, I trust you, just making sure."

Rene raised his hand to stop me from saying anything further. We did a high-five through the bulletproof glass. Elena had suggested to run over and win Graham over, to let him meet me. Maybe it was good to go personally. I headed off in my car, bracing myself for that meeting at the bank, Mr. Graham, in person. It was the first time I met the no-nonsense banker, Graham. He actually smiled, but that was just window dressing. I settled in the chair across the desk from Graham instead of Holmberg. It didn't feel quite right. We shook hands over the top of the desk.

George Hatcher

"If you have this much, why didn't you deposit it before the check came in?"

"That's a good question. I have no excuse," I said. "I promise I will make banking my priority. The shop is busy, and frankly, I get distracted."

Graham stared. I met his gaze squarely.

"I paid the check after you told me you were coming right over with a deposit."

"I'm indebted. Thank you."

It was strange to see Holmberg's office without Holmberg in it. Connie was still out there where she had been for years. I did not see Holmberg's pictures on the desk. I didn't know Graham's people, but I didn't see any of his pictures either. I tried to look without looking like I was looking.

"Take the deposit to the teller," he said. He stood up. I took the cue and stood. We shook hands again.

* * *

Back at the shop, I filled out the check stub for the thirteen thousand seventy-five I cashed at Rene's and crossed out the fifteen thousand from my desk plotter. I added the new check I wrote Rene to get the cash.

"I know how it works," Elena said. "That doesn't stop me from being amazed. You went back to Rene to cash a check, then drove to the bank with his cash to cover his check that was causing an overdraft at your bank."

"Well, I could have gone to Chester to get the thirteen thousand I was short, but I figured Rene knew his check could bounce because his employee deposited it earlier than we had agreed."

"Amazing," Elena said. "Do you think this is legal?"

"I think it's totally legal until a check starts bouncing, then we have insufficient funds. Years ago, at the county, I met guys who were waiting for trial for writing checks for non-sufficient funds."

Elena shook her head.

I didn't know that the district attorney could file grand theft charges when there is evidence of more than one transaction. If you go to a department store, write a check for a hundred dollars, and it bounces, you could be charged with insufficient funds, a crime but not a huge crime. If you write a check for a hundred dollars to more than one store, then it is possible the prosecutor can try to convict you for grand theft. I got convicted of grand theft over the loan from Thelma that I did not payback. Getting convicted of grand theft carries a stiffer sentence than insufficient funds.

When my accountant wrote the month-end checks, he did so from my account at Kitty's bank. My account for Mike's shop, Whittier Auto Center, was also at Kitty's bank, but I never wrote checks from that account. Mike handled it on his own.

Like before, when Donald left the shop, he would tell me how much I needed to deposit before I mailed out the checks he had written. The only difference was that my deposits were being made at Kitty's bank. It became my primary bank. I preferred dealing with Kitty over Graham.

Graham was a man I had lots of misgivings for. It didn't matter that he was only doing his job. I was a customer with an outstanding record of paying my loans, and he was rude to me. I overdrew my account, but only because Holmberg said he'd cover me. At the time, my brain was focused on my bank relationships and keeping my credit good.

* * *

I was at the Latin Playboy Bar nursing a beer and fantasizing about James' wife, Molly, who was the server behind the bar. I got there right at four when she started. Only three people were at the bar. She attended to the others first, then came over to talk to me. I was speaking barely loud enough for her to hear. Music was playing all the time.

"Do you smoke?"

"I don't smoke," I said, "How about you?"

"One a day," she said.

"Are you married?"

"I'm married. About to get a divorce," I said.

"Too bad."

"Not bad. It's been pending for a very long time. I have a daughter and a son. We were waiting for my son to be born."

"Why?"

I shrugged. "It happens."

"I know," she said. "I'm seriously thinking of divorcing James."

"That's too bad."

"No, it's not. He wants a wife, but he's out all the time messing around with other women."

I wondered if Molly knew about Adrian.

"That's too bad. I mean, you're gorgeous. Why would he want to fool around with anyone else?"

That was so bad of me. I'm such a hypocrite.

"You think I'm gorgeous?"

"Absolutely. Don't you know how gorgeous you are?"

"What?" she asked, cupping her hand over her ear like funneling my voice would make it clearer.

Molly moved up close, an inch from my face. I repeated myself. The tavern door opened, revealing Brooklyn Avenue traffic for the length of time it took for the door to fall closed. Elena walked in.

"Hey," I said, waving my arm so she could see me.

"Hi," Elena said.

"This is Molly," I said. "Molly, this is Elena."

They smiled at each other.

"Can I get you something to drink?"

Elena shook her head. "I wish. I have a herd of people at the shop picking up their cars. Maybe some other time."

Elena moved close and whispered, "You had a call from Kitty. She wants you to call her back before the bank closes. I thought you'd want to know."

"Sure. I'll walk back with you," I said, getting off the stool and putting a five-dollar bill on the counter. Elena had her back to me and was walking toward the door. "Thanks, Molly, see you soon."

Molly waved.

We waited for the traffic to slow. Standing at the curb, Elena said, "Now I understand why you come over here every day."

"I never even finish one beer."

Elena gave me a playful shove. "You are not there for the beer, Babe. You're a womanizer from the get-go."

"I know," I admitted. "I'm sorry."

She shoved me again, still playful. As we walked into the shop, we split like the Red Sea. She headed to a waiting customer, and I went up to the office to call Kitty.

Elena was driving us home from the shop. She pulled out of the parking lot and into traffic. Her eyes were on the fifty-eight red Chevy in front of us, whose driver was riding his brakes.

"She's very pretty," Elena said, without taking her eyes from the traffic.

"You mean Molly."

"I ain't talking 'bout that Chevy up there being driven by lead-foot," she said. "Baby, stop the innocent act."

"Yeah, she's very pretty."

I reached over and touched the back of Elena's neck. It must have given her a chill because she shivered.

"She's married," I said.

"So are you."

"Ouch."

"Well, you are. I met her husband, James, before," Elena said.

"Really? How did you meet him?"

"He came over to fix his car, remember?"

"Oh yeah. It was you that gave him the quote to repair his spot paint job."

"Right. I introduced you to the neighbor who owns the Latin Playboy next door."

"I remember."

"You missed him making three passes at me, two when I explained the charge to repair, and once when he came to pick up the car."

"Did he tell you he was married?"

"I asked him. He said he was married with a little girl."

"What did you tell him?"

"I told him I don't date customers. He asked if being married made a difference."

"And what did you say to that?"

"I told him I wasn't dating at the moment. He said, 'Lucky whoever it is.'"

"Baby, you are a flirt," I reminded her.

"Look who's talking." She laughed.

"Baby, I love you already."

She gave me a sideways look. We were silent all the way home. I thought of Molly.

We never wore pajamas, button-downs, or righteous pajamas, but that night, we did. It's why I remember that night. I had several from the locker thing that I'd never put on before, but they were nice. Elena had a beautiful burgundy set that I figured would be uncomfortable to sleep in because it fit her snugly, revealing her anatomy.

On nights like this, I wished I hadn't given up the great house. Elena brought out the vine-etched glasses, clear long-stemmed graceful. We sat in the living room.

She poured the glasses halfway full, and we touched the rims with a tiny clink. I sipped slowly, loving the complicated, rich flavor of the Boudreaux. We brought the wine and our glasses into the kitchen to prep a chopping block loaded with cheese and all the trimmings that would be our dinner.

We sat at the kitchen table across from each other, the chopping block between us. Elena poured Boudreaux.

"I'm going to take a half day off tomorrow," she said.

"Why half? Take the whole day off. You work like crazy."

She bit into a dried fig. "Baby, don't get dramatic."

"Okay, half day, whole day. You've earned it," I said, going for the cheese.

"I'm going to the salon to do the works and probably my hair."

"I love your hair," I said.

She tilted her head forward, and her straight, dark pageboy moved with her. Her hair was really spectacular. It fit her.

"You like blondes. Donna in Vegas and now Molly, both blondes."

"Oh baby, I shouldn't be so truthful." That got a stare at me.

"The best quality you have is that you tell the truth," she said. "Don't change that."

"Is that the only good quality?"

"I'm mad at you, or I'd compliment you more."

"Baby, you can't get mad at me."

"I can if I want to."

Elena wasn't really mad at me. I think she was hurt when she saw Molly. Susie was a doll. Alexa was a doll. She had met Clara, a knockout. It wasn't the pretty in Molly that was the danger. She saw Molly as a threat to our relationship. That moment she spent in the tavern was long enough for Elena to question our relationship from then on.

* * *

Elena came from the beauty shop with a stunning short pixie cut. I immediately wanted to roll around with her and play with her hair as she played with mine.

Susie and Alexa hugged her.

"I dig it. Is it okay if I get your stylist to do my hair the same way?" Susie asked.

"Sure," Elena said.

"I love it," Alexa said.

I wanted to devour her right there and then.

"I've been cutting my own hair for seven years," Elena said to all of us. "The dude that did this has it totally together. I love what he did."

"Baby let's go to the office, and I'll show you how much I love it," I said.

Elena shunned my pass.

I shunned her at ten after four when I walked across the street to the Latin Playboy to fantasize about the mystery of a married woman.

I came back through the Rowan entrance after drinking my half beer. Only the paint department saw me come in.

* * *

I drove us home. We stopped at the Hat after not being there for a long time. Maybe I should have taken Elena out to dinner on the other side of town like we did that time we brought Susie. There was no reason not to. The cost of a meal, no matter how expensive, was a drop in the bottomless hole I was in any way.

We shared pastrami and a tamale. We had plenty of room for some delicious wine. Elena was no longer complaining about the drinking. A bottle of wine with both of us drinking was good for three nights. Priests drink more than that on their own.

"I can't wait to get you home," I said in the car on the way home. "I want to devour you. The new hair is great on you. I love it."

She reached over and pulled my curls. "You can't devour me too much. It's that time."

I turned to look at her in the darkened car. "Doesn't matter," I said.

"Yeah, it matters, chicken." She laughed.

* * *

At home, we cuddled together on the sofa. Music was playing. We were toying with our glasses of wine, watching the lamplight shine through the burgundy.

"G, the lady is married," Elena said. "What are you doing going over there every day? I'm not asking because I'm jealous."

"You answered for me. She's married. What could I be doing?"

"Bull, G. I know you."

I raised my glass. It took her a moment to raise hers and click.

* * *

The cook next door made Elena a hot beef sandwich on homemade bread. I was having Carne Asada smothered with red salsa, not very spicy, just enough.

"Baby, I need to spring for a little while," Elena said.

I stopped eating. She had already stopped. We're looking at each other across the table in my office.

"You said you wouldn't leave me again," I said.

"I'm not moving out. I'm only going to spring away for a little while."

"Where you going?"

"I'm not sure."

"Is it because of Molly? If it is, there is nothing there, and you know it."

"It's not Molly."

"Then why?"

She shrugged, giving me no explanation. For a second or two, I thought of walking out, but how stupid would that have been? She took another bite. I started eating.

"Her husband is a kind of gangster," Elena said lightly. "Or maybe it's his brothers. You know how this neighborhood is. Gossip is that he is kind of dirty."

I shrugged. "I was in prison with a whole bunch of gangsters." I chuckled. "Besides, I'm not doing anything with his wife."

"Baby, I meant nothing. I only want you to be careful. Plenty of women out there aren't married. If you are tired of me, go get one of them."

I stopped eating. She wouldn't look at me.

"I'm not tired of you," I said. "Maybe it's the other way around."

"Think what you must," she said. "If it bothers you, I'll move my clothes to my aunt's."

I reached across the table and took her free hand. She looked up.

"Come back, hopefully soon. I'll give you money."

"Baby, you know I don't need money. Thank you just the same."

In the morning, I jogged alone.

* * *

When I closed the shop that night, I didn't ask Susie to go home with me. I had never made a pass at Alexa. I went home alone. I didn't have dinner, and I didn't drink. I did go to the Latin Playboy, but I barely was able to chat with Molly because she was so busy. It was a fucked-up day. I went to bed earlier than I could remember. I found myself lying there, waiting for sleep. I thought of how great it would be if Elena showed up as she'd done in the past.

Elena didn't show up.

* * *

Elena checked in by phone on Friday morning.

"I'm in New York."

"How neat is that?" I said that to her.

"David has an apartment here. I'll give you the phone number when you're ready."

"David. Do I know him?"

"Baby, it's the Texan. His name is David Marks. I told you before."

"Okay, got it. Give me the phone number."

She gave it to me, but I didn't write it down. Why would I want to call her in New York at the Texan's house? No reason at all.

That night, I went home alone again. I knew it would be close to impossible to get Emma or Ava to come over because it was Friday, but I tried anyway.

Emma picked up.

"You must not be working?"

"Doesn't happen often, but it happened tonight. I had an all-nighter who didn't show. Jaimie is working on the hit-and-run type. What you doing?"

"Call Jaimie and tell him I want you for the night. Let me know what I have to give him so he doesn't press you."

"Are you sure you want to pay him?"

"Emma, just do it. I don't want to get in another fight with that bastard."

Because it was a Friday, Jaimie wanted seventy-five, plus I had to take care of Emma. I agreed. She came over.

"Want to do something different before we fuck?" she asked.

"I'm all ears, Emma."

"Let's go clubbing. You ever been to West LA?"

"I have, but it was a long time ago. Where to?"

"I hear that P.J.'s is sweet. I ain't been there, but I hear it's fun."

"I'm game," I said. "But I can't drink unless we take a taxi."

"Are you serious?"

"Serious as serious."

"Let's stay here. I'll cook you something."

"No, let's go to P.J.'s. We'll take a taxi there, let our hair down, and take a taxi back."

"I need a half-hour to get ready. Just put on a pair of slacks, a shirt, and no tennis shoes. You might or might not need a jacket, but I will call about the jacket to be sure. My friend told me dressy casual."

"I'll wear a sports jacket. Hurry back."

Chapter 14
P.J.'s Discotheque

We took a Yellow Cab. PJ's was nothing like the clubs I had been to with Christina or Selena. I was in slacks and my sports jacket. Emma was in a crazy red top that had white dots going down the front like buttons. The matching white skirt had red buttons going down the rest of the way. Her shoes were red flats with a strap, with a huge white daisy on the toe. I bet when she got it, it was much longer, but I remember Ava saying that they always hemmed their dresses because skirts were always getting shorter.

I love short and it was fine with me that skirts kept getting shorter.

PJ's was brand-new and very different from the clubs I'd been to. It was the first Disco in Los Angeles. If I had brought it, my Chevy would have been the only one amongst the limousines, sports cars, and Cadillacs. My Chevy was new and hot, but the club's clientele was made up of money people. I bet Emma and I were the only East Los Angeles couple there, but no one would know we weren't in the right place.

It was the first time in ages that I ordered CC Water. There was a wine list, but we didn't feel like doing the wine glass thing in a jumping joint like this one, action, live band, dancing non-stop. I'm no dancer, but back then, I didn't let that stop me,

When the band took a break, the background music settled down, and we could actually hear each other.

"I could make a killing here tonight," Emma said.

I wasn't mad or anything, but I'd had a few drinks. I knew Emma was a working girl.

"Baby go for it if you want," I said.

"I was kidding, G."

"You weren't kidding." I laughed.

It was still early. I slowed down on my drinks, unsure if I still cared for hard liquor after being off of it for so long. I nursed my drinks like I nursed the beer Molly served me at the tavern.

Emma was on her second dance with a guy older than she was.

I'm not shy, but I was out of touch with having a social life. My social life was back at my apartment. I felt awkward and out of step, like I had just gotten out of prison. I played with my drink. I saw a girl sitting at a table alone like I was. I walked over in a thundercloud of noise. It would have been pointless to speak. I extended my hand. She smiled, took my hand, and we joined the couples on the crowded dance floor. The dance was fast. It was easier for me to stay relaxed.

The music was hot. This girl could dance, and she tried to get me to move like she was moving. It was funny. We were both laughing, but no one was listening or watching. It was like it was just her and me. She had red patent leather shoes that matched her outfit. Her skirt was tight and short.

She was a brunette. In this light, her eyes looked brown, but with the lighting, I couldn't really tell much. Our third dance without sitting down was a slow one. Slow was so much easier for me. I kept my distance.

She broke the ice by stroking my hair.

"I love your hair," she said. "My name is Kathy, with a K."

She was there with two friends, Harlow and Candace. The band took a break, and we were able to talk and hear each other better.

I kept looking for Emma, but she was nowhere to be found. I told Kathy that I'd come with a neighbor who had disappeared.

"I'm not sorry your date split and left you here for me," she said.

I figured Emma would show.

The three of them lived in the San Fernando Valley. Kathy's friend, Harlow, wanted me to explain where Monterey Hills was located.

"About thirty miles from where you live."

"No P.J.'s there?" asked Candace.

"No," I said. "This is one of a kind."

P.J.'s was cozy, dark, and intimate, a disco with wood paneling, checkered tablecloths, low lighting, and a band. Before the band's next set, we saw a hysterical musical puppet show called Les Poupées de Paris.

Kathy said, "We come every week."

The three ladies were all married. Not to each other, though that was my first thought. My second thought was of Molly. I wished she wasn't married. When I heard Kathy was also married, I wondered what I was doing there.

Emma was somewhere, and I was entangled with three married ladies. Emma had turned me on to the P.J.'s. and I could bring Elena here. We needed to get out more. And if she didn't come back soon enough, fuck it. I'd come alone.

Kathy asked, "Do you need a ride?"

"I came here in a taxi and plan to take a cab back home," I said.

"We don't drink and drive either," Candace said. "We have a hired driver and car outside."

"Smart," I said.

In the hours I spent at P.J.'s, first with Emma and later with Kathy and her friends, I never thought of my business problems.

Guys asked Kathy and her friends to dance. They danced away. I danced with total strangers. None of the girls I asked to dance rejected me. The whole experience was cool and new to me. At one in the morning, I was in Kathy's hired SUV headed to Canter's Deli on Fairfax. I'd never been to this Canter's, but we had one on Brooklyn Avenue in East Los Angeles where I met up with Sam. The one the girls took me to was a place screen, and television stars frequented after hours.

Kathy and I exchanged phone numbers at the deli. She whispered, "I'm home all day. I don't work. I have no kids. When you feel like it, call me. We can have lunch, go somewhere, and kick back."

"I'd love that," I said. "What if your husband answers?"

"He won't, but if he does, ask for me."

She was lovely.

"When did you all meet?" I asked.

They giggled like schoolgirls.

"We met forever ago."

"We were in diapers, I think."

"Lifelong gal pals. After high school, we got married-"

"Not to each other!" Kathy interrupted. They all broke out in laughter.

It was amazing to me that they didn't have kids yet. They acted like they were living by a pact they'd made among themselves (though I could be reading something into it.) I didn't have that part of the story.

I took a cab from Canter's and slept all the way home. I was not the least bit drunk but just used to rising early. I felt good. I entered by the front of the apartment building, where the cab dropped me off. When I put the key in the door, Emma came running to me from her apartment. She was out of her disco gear and in grey sweats.

"Where you been, G? I was worried about you. It's 3:15."

I laughed.

"You crazy? The question is, where were you, Emma?"

She pinched my butt. I opened the door, and we both walked into my apartment.

"I owe you, G. You got anything you want. I already took care of Jaime."

I figured she scored at P.J.'s, but that was her business. I scored two. I found out about P.J.'s, and I made three new friends. They were married, but that was okay. I planned to call Kathy.

* * *

It's fair to say that I got very little sleep. I didn't jog, woke up, hit the shower, drove to the shop, and opened on time.

Suddenly I missed Elena big time. In spite of everything I did the night before, I missed Elena. Maybe I was crazy. Maybe she was an addiction.

I had my lunch at eleven in the morning. Susie picked up a perfectly cooked Rib-Eye steak from the meat market and served it to me on a large porcelain plate covered with aluminum foil. It was only me there, but I was sitting at the table for two in my office that Elena had bought for us to have lunch on.

"You should have ordered something," I told Susie.

"It's early, but I thank you. Can I get something else for you?"

"I'm good for now," I said. "Thanks, Susie."

"Take a snooze, Boss. We can handle it downstairs."

"I might do that. Thanks."

I ate, and then the lack of sleep hit me. I didn't intend to crash on the sofa, but I was full, then bam, it was hours later, and Alexa was leaning over me with her hand on my shoulder. Maybe she was shaking me.

"Elena on the phone," she said.

"Wha???"

"Boss, it's Elena. She's on the phone, long-distance."

Eventually, I comprehended what was being said.

"Tell her I'm asleep," I said.

"Will do, G, sorry I woke you."

* * *

Of course, I called Kathy to see if she'd like to go out for lunch.

"If you game, there's a Hilton on Ventura Boulevard in Encino. We can order room service. Only if you game," she said with a little cough.

I was game, all right. It didn't matter to me or apparently to her that she was married. I didn't know her husband. What Kathy and I did that day was a routine anything goes act of the sixties sexual revolution that had taken over California and much of the country.

The Hilton on Ventura Boulevard in Encino was nice, but I wasn't there for the décor. Apart from the cool grubby sex, her conversation was interesting, even enlightening. Up close and personal, Kathy was a fox and a sexual adventurer. Twice a month, Kathy, Candace, and Harlow swapped husbands. She told me all about it.

"I don't believe it."

She laughed at my naiveté. "I don't know what you do in Monterey Hills," she said, "but in the Valley where we live, wife swapping is a thing. Everyone does it."

Maybe that's why they had a pact or something about not having children yet. Kathy never gave me those details.

"Where did you learn to take care of a woman like you do?" she asked before we kissed goodbye.

I thought of Christine. "I don't remember," I lied.

As I drove back to the main shop, the sight of the bustling building stirred a mix of nostalgia and uncertainty within me. Inside, mechanics were hard at work, and customers flowed in and out, some seeking estimates, others dropping off or picking up their cars. There was no denying it—I had struck gold with this first shop. But the other locations told a different story. They were bleeding me dry, barely breaking even, and I couldn't sustain them any longer.

Letting go felt monumental—a daunting idea that weighed heavily on my heart. After more than four years of struggle, the thought of closing one or more of my shops was almost unbearable. The dream I'd fought for was now a bittersweet burden.

Alexa

Saturday night, I asked Susie and Alexa if they wanted to go to P.J.'s. I explained it was a nightclub on the West Side. They said they'd love it. I told them what not to wear: no jeans, no tennis shoes, anything dressy casual worked.

Pages of Passion Book 4: Threads of Destiny

Susie

Alexa had a car. She picked up Susie at home and then drove to my house. She parked in a guest spot under the building, and I met them in the garage. We split from there in my car. I didn't plan on having more than a drink or two, and the booze would be spaced out, so no way would I not be sober when I drove home.

Susie and Alexa loved the place, just as I had. They were asked to dance one time after another. That was okay. I hit the dance floor.

We got to my apartment after two Sunday morning. I offered the girls the second bedroom, and I really didn't care if they took me up on it or if they left and didn't stay over. I guess that's what made for a great night.

Susie said, "I'll stay, but I want to sleep with you, Boss."

"Got room for me?" Alexa asked. I had never been with her before.

Back then, sex was so uncomplicated.

Chapter 15
Elena Returns

Elena sprang back after eleven days after she left.

"How was New York?"

"Beautiful but cold. Too cold for me."

"Chilly here as well," I said.

"Baby, no comparison."

I had never been to New York. I had to take her word for it. I did not ask about the Texan, and she volunteered nothing about her trip.

I didn't talk about what I'd done while she was gone, like making three new friends at P.J.'s, like my lunch 'date' with Kathy, like taking Alexa and Susie to P.J.'s, and especially like being at the tavern for half an hour at a few minutes past four when Molly was serving.

* * *

Meanwhile, back at Eastland Auto Center, Sam let me know we had hit the hundred thousand mark. He had loaned my shops about eighty-three thousand, and he was owed one hundred thousand.

"Sam, you know I never snivel, but I thought your ceiling meant you were out of pocket one hundred thousand. You're out of pocket eighty-three thousand, not a hundred.

Sam laughed. He was a great sport.

"Georgie, okay, I'll go along with that. Once we hit one hundred thousand out of pocket, the bank is closed until the money comes in to reduce the debt."

"Got it," I said.

I let Mike know how close we had come close to getting cut off.

"That means we only have seventeen thousand in borrowing power."

At about the same time, Chester was on the local television news. He had been held up. The details were not clear yet. I had not talked to him. The news report said the robber had gotten away with eighty-thousand dollars that the gas station used to cash checks for customers.

I tried calling the gas station, but there was no answer. I could have walked over there but didn't. I figured Chester would call me. He did better than call. The day after the news, he showed up at the shop.

"Are you okay?" The first thing I said.

He, Elena, and I went up to my office.

"I'm fine. The cops interrogated me for hours. Right off, I was the suspect. I was given two lie detector tests, the first for the cops and the second for the insurance investigators. I told my boss to shove it. I quit this morning. I can't work for someone who doesn't trust me. I quit, and I feel better already."

"Did you pass the test?" Elena asked.

"Elena, I didn't rob myself. Yes, I passed, or they would have me in jail right now."

"Where were you robbed?"

"It was one guy with a stocking mask. It happened right as I got out of my car five feet from the door to the cubicle where no one could get me."

"Did he have a gun like the news said?" I asked.

"He had a forty-five."

"Were you scared?" Elena asked.

"Hell yes, I was scared. I told the dude to take the money and leave me be."

Elena laughed and gave Chester a hug right there on the sofa.

"Did you give him five minutes before you sounded the alarm?"

"It took me longer than five minutes to recover from the shock."

Chester laughed, then Elena and I joined him.

With Chester quitting his job, the twelve thousand in checks he was holding would be deposited that day immediately by the person who was taking over his job. I had to get twelve thousand in my account at Kitty's bank in not more than four days to prevent an overdraft.

"I'm going home for a couple of weeks," Chester said. "My mom and dad are in Missouri. Can I leave my car here? I want it to be safe, and I figure here is safe if you can find a place inside."

"We have a spot for it," Elena said.

"Yeah, for sure," I said. "We'll look after the car."

"Chester, did you stash eighty thousand in your car?" Elena asked.

Chester got all serious. "I wish," he said.

We laughed it off.

Chester took a cab home to pack, and then he'd be off in the morning. We offered him a ride, but he said it was not necessary.

"I wish all the check cashers would stop cashing my checks," I said. "I'd find a less stressful way to take care of the shortages."

"Baby, rule out Vegas."

I exhaled slowly, something I do. "I'm not going to Vegas."

* * *

I went to Rene's Check Cashing, and the owner let me in the iron door to the back where Rene's office was located.

"My bank is asking me to explain checks that don't appear to be paychecks. Your checks. Big checks like fifteen thousand, in the past eight thousand. My bank can't tell me how to run my business, but they can put holds on my account for large checks. If I don't get immediate credit like I've always got, I'm dead."

"My checks have never bounced," I said.

"If even one had bounced, the banker would take a hard look at what I deposit."

"Are you saying you can't cash checks anymore?"

"Not at all. Change the size of the checks. If you need ten thousand, don't bring me one check to hold. Bring me forty checks for two fifty. Make them out to any name you want, endorse them, and I'll cash them as before. I'll hold them as before."

How many times had I told myself that nothing lasts forever?

"I got it, Rene."

I shook his hand and left. It was just as well the rules were changing. I was there with a check for eight thousand with plans to head for Vegas. Elena didn't know. No one knew. I went back to the shop with my tail between my legs. I would have to order a whole lot of blank checks to do as Rene wanted. The good thing was that three other check cashing places had not made that rule. Mike had some places as well. The bad thing is if I was floating big money, I would need more check cashing places than I had. I couldn't count Mike's because he was carrying himself at Whittier Auto Center.

"Let's go home," I said to Elena. We were on the shop floor. "I need a swim or something. Maybe if I'm lucky, I'll drown."

Elena laughed. "Baby, you go. We got you covered."

"You won't have a car," I said.

"I hear Alexa knows the way. She can take me after we close."

Elena had learned that Susie and Alexa had been with me while she was in New York, but she didn't seem to care. She knew I had never been with Alexa before that.

"I'll call you," I said, kissing Elena and heading for my car.

Elena took her job seriously. I could only admire her work ethic. She left when she wanted, but when she was working, she didn't lose focus. We were busy, and the shop needed her. That's why she didn't go home with me.

Less than half an hour later, I was in the heated pool. It was chilly out, so I was alone. No one else was crazy enough to get in. Ava saw me out there and came out of her apartment to investigate. She was wearing long sleeves and a sweater.

"You crazy?"

"It's heated. You know that. Come in, and I'll warm you up."

* * *

It was early afternoon, so I was surprised that Ava was up already. She invited me over, but I was so disturbed by business events that I couldn't get it up. I wrapped up in the towel I had taken to and from the pool. I was on their sofa with Ava between my legs when Emma spontaneously appeared, smiling, yawning, and helping Ava. Mission failed. I kissed them, walked across to my apartment, crashed on my bed, and then jumped out of it to turn on the heat.

When I woke up, it was after five. I had missed seeing Molly at the tavern. Damn. Sometimes, she wasn't there. Maybe she didn't work that shift today. I hadn't seen Adrian lately. To see her, I'd have to come earlier. She worked noon to four and eight to close. Noon wasn't convenient, and by eight at night, I was home. My life was a routine.

Elena burst through the door, her arms laden with steaming hot bags of hamburgers, crispy golden fries, and spicy chili tamales that filled the room with an intoxicating aroma.

"Who brought you?" I asked, my curiosity piqued.

"Alexa and Susie dropped me off and left. Is that okay, or did you want them here?" she replied, her eyes sparkling with mischief.

I wrapped my arm around her, feeling the warmth of her body through her clothes, and guided her to the kitchen, my hand resting possessively on her firm backside. I couldn't help but notice that my excitement, which had been dormant with Ava and Emma, was now unmistakably alive.

"A quickie before we eat," I suggested, my voice low and teasing, "unless you don't want to."

Elena set the bags down on the table with a decisive thud, then grabbed my erection and tugged me towards the bedroom with a playful urgency, like a dog eager for a walk.

Later, we devoured the feast, the flavors exploding in our mouths, each bite a symphony of taste and texture. Elena then uncorked a bottle of Rothschild Bordeaux, a thirty-five-dollar treasure from the early sixties, which would be a small fortune today. She let it breathe, the rich, velvety aroma filling the air, before pouring a glass and offering it to me. I took a sip, the complex flavors dancing on my tongue, but I knew she was the true connoisseur. I nodded in appreciation.

We moved to the living room, sinking into the plush sofa, our glasses in hand. We sipped and gazed at each other, the soft glow of the lamp casting a warm light on our faces. It was a picture of contentment, yet something felt off, an imperfection I couldn't quite place.

The next morning, our routine remained unbroken. We jogged through the crisp morning air, the rhythmic sound of our feet hitting the pavement in sync. After a refreshing shower, we dressed and sat down for our ritualistic John Wayne coffee—delicious, black, and strong, its bold flavor waking us up with each sip. Sometimes we'd indulge in pan dulce, its sweet, flaky goodness a perfect complement, but today, Elena hadn't picked any up at the meat market.

Chapter 16
The Unspeakable Truth

The shop phone shrieked, slicing through the usual morning chatter and laughter of customers dropping off cars. It was just after opening, and the four of us were buzzing with activity, a fleeting moment of ordinary life. The phone rang again, a frantic, insistent demand for attention. I sprinted to the nearest wall phone, snatching up the receiver.

Sophia's voice, my wife's voice, was a strangled, broken sound on the other end, barely audible through her sobs. "George... Leonie choked on his milk. I... I don't think he's going to make it."

Time didn't just freeze; it shattered. My world imploded. Then, Sophia's grandfather's voice, shockingly steady amidst the chaos, cut through the static of my terror. "Get over here, George." It wasn't a request; it was an order, an urgent beacon in the sudden, crushing darkness.

I slammed the receiver back into its cradle, the clang echoing like a gunshot in my ears. The customer standing before me, mid-sentence, became an invisible blur. I didn't apologize, couldn't even speak. I bolted for my car, my lungs burning, each breath a struggle. Elena, startled by my sudden flight, chased after me, her footsteps pounding behind, her concern a palpable wave of panic.

"My son," I gasped, wrenching open the car door. "He choked... critical. I have to go." The words caught in my throat, mirroring the horror I imagined for my baby.

"Oh my God. Let me drive you!" she cried, her own voice rising with fear.

But I was already moving, jamming the car into reverse. The tires screamed as I slammed the pedal, tearing out of the parking lot like a bat out of hell, leaving everything behind—the shop, the customers, Elena's desperate plea.

"Let this be a nightmare. Or if it's real, let him live. Please, God, let him live." My thoughts were a frantic, desperate prayer, a torrent of familiar pleas to the Virgin of Guadalupe, to God, to any power that might listen. A molten rage began to bubble beneath the fear. How? How could my son, my perfect, precious Leonie, have choked while drinking from his bottle? It was an absurdity, a cruel twist of fate I couldn't comprehend.

As I neared Sophia's grandparents' place, the sight hit me like a physical blow. Fire engines, their sirens now muted, paramedics swarming the street, red and white lights flashing like a macabre dance. The very traffic itself felt like an ominous, sluggish omen, each stopped car a barrier, mocking my desperate urgency.

I burst through the front door. The air inside was thick with unspoken grief, a suffocating weight. I found Sophia, her face tear-streaked and hollow, and pulled her into a fierce embrace. Our cries mingled, a primal duet of sorrow that enveloped us both like a heavy, inescapable shroud. The tears flowed, hot and endless, but so did the rage. I felt utterly, completely betrayed. God had taken him. It wasn't Sophia's fault; she hadn't even heard him choke. No, this was on God. He had allowed it to happen. He had stolen my son.

Leonie was not even six months old when he passed away. His tiny grave now rests at Calvary Cemetery in East Los Angeles, just to the right as you enter the main gates, near what used to be the old office. In the raw, agonizing wake of this tragedy, Sophia's family did their best to shield my young daughter, Judy. She was just a baby, innocently unaware of the storm that had not just shattered our lives, but utterly destroyed a piece of my soul.

Chapter 17
Downward Spiral

In the unbearable darkness that followed my son's death, Elena tried to be an anchor. She showed up day after day, a lifeline I couldn't quite grasp. Mike was a comforting shadow, but I resisted them both like a drowning man fighting off a rescuer. I craved the punishing embrace of solitude and silence. My apartment, once a refuge, became a prison. The air grew thick with the smell of stale beer and regret, a bottle of Canadian Club my only constant companion as I slid deeper into the abyss.

While I was lost in my grief-fueled haze, the financial time bombs I had set continued to tick. Fifty-nine thousand dollars in checks I had floated to various outlets, including Rene, were deposited on their agreed-upon dates. Elena saw the cryptic notes on my desk, but the chaotic ledger of my check-kiting scheme was a language only I understood. You had to be me to know what the hell it all meant, and at that moment, I barely knew myself.

Vicki called the shop, then the apartment. I never answered. Elena, bless her heart, kept making deposits to Kitty's bank, but she was in the dark, unaware of the tidal wave of checks about to crash against an empty account. The deposits she made were a handful of sand against a tsunami.

Then the wave hit. Kitty bounced fifty thousand dollars in checks.

The first call came from a furious check-cashing manager. Elena answered. I can only imagine the horror as the gravity of the situation hit her like a ton of bricks. In that one angry phone call, she understood it all—the kiting, the massive debt, the house of cards I had built. Fueled by a desperate mix of anger and concern, she immediately called Kitty, unleashing a torrent of fury while revealing the full, devastating context of the crisis: the death of my son.

Later, I told Elena it wouldn't have made a difference. My son's death wasn't supposed to open a new line of credit for me to pay the fucking checks. Yet, she stayed. Day after day, she went to work. Night after night, she came home to a man who was disappearing into a bottle. Looking back, it's a miracle she remained by my side.

My mourning had twisted into something ugly. The sorrow for my son morphed into a searing anger at myself for the scarce moments I had shared with him, for the father I hadn't been. Overwhelmed by fury and remorse, I hurled blame at God, then despised myself for doing so. I was a shattered soul, lost in a maelstrom of my own making.

Then, one morning, something shifted. Maybe God got tired of ignoring me and decided to throw me a rope. I woke up, and through the fog of a wicked hangover, I saw the wreckage of my apartment and my life. After Elena left for the shop, I shaved, stood under the shower until the water ran cold, and got dressed. I was stone-cold sober and swore to myself I would stay that way. As I drove to the shop, the clarity was terrifying. I knew I was in deep, deep trouble.

Friday was payday. The account at Kitty's Bank was a black hole. I couldn't write checks. Just before noon, I called my employees at the main shop into my office. They barely fit, a nervous crowd packed into the small room perched precariously above the meat market's walk-in coolers. I feared the weight of their collective anxiety, and my own, might send us all crashing down.

"I'm going to have to close this shop," I began, the words tasting like poison. "I'm going to write every one of you a check. I want you to go cash them, but don't go to the bank. Use a check-cashing place. If they bounce, they will come to me, not you."

Elena immediately offered to loan me her savings, but I couldn't take her money. I couldn't go back to my parents. This was my mess. My employees, to my astonishment, didn't want me to shut down. It was Elena who came up with the desperate, brilliant plan. Stop paying bills. Stop making deposits. Pay everyone in cash next week. For now, she asked, how much did each person need to get by?

I watched, numb and detached, as she and Susie organized it all. I had twenty-one employees, including the upholsterers I carried on my books out of loyalty. Elena and Susie arranged for Jesse and Chris next door to prepare a care package of groceries for each family. Each employee was given twenty dollars in cash and an IOU for the rest of their week's pay. Nothing was deducted. And in that moment, when they should have all walked out, not a single person quit. Not one complained. They stood by me.

I had come full circle. I was following in the footsteps of Ramirez, my predecessor, running a business on fumes and desperation. My credit would be shot. My vendors would put me on C.O.D. I looked at the loyalty of my team, the chaos of my finances, and the gaping hole in my heart, and all I could think was, *Fuck it.*

That evening, when I walked into my apartment, it was spotless. The stale air of grief and alcohol was gone, replaced by the scent of lemon oil. The kitchen gleamed, the bed had fresh linens, the bathrooms shone. It couldn't have been Elena; she'd been at the shop with me all day. Then the phone rang. It was Ava and Emma.

"It wasn't easy breaking in without breaking something," Ava's voice chimed through the receiver, "but we hope you like the way it looks."

I wanted to cry. When Elena got home with takeout, I finally broke. I thanked her for everything, for the days and nights she had put up with me, and the tears I had held back for so long finally came. It was the last time Elena would ever see me cry.

The next morning, I was up before her. I stepped out into the cold air to jog, loving the sharp sting on my face. I was out of shape; a sick body implodes quickly. I thought of the hangovers, of the promises I'd made to myself before. This time had to be different. I was done with hard liquor. I was done being a drunk. I had to climb out of the abyss, one painful step at a time.

With our bank accounts decimated, the business had to adapt instantly. Few customers paid by check anymore; we started politely requesting cash when they dropped off their cars, and strictly demanded it for pickup. Credit cards were still a distant dream for auto repair. There were no more bank deposits. No more paying bills with checks. On payday, I personally handed out envelopes stuffed with cash, covering the current week and whatever arrears we had. Elena, ever selfless, refused hers, but I left it on my desk, a silent battle of wills. Everyone at the Car Wash Shop and Soto Street also received their cash.

That same Friday, four insurance checks arrived in the mail. I didn't dare deposit them into my now-toxic account. Instead, I endorsed them and drove straight to Sam's store.

"I'm having problems," I admitted, laying the checks on

his counter. "I've endorsed these over to you. Kitty will accept them for deposit into your account, I'm sure."

Sam looked at me, his expression softening. "I heard about your son, Georgie. Please accept my deepest condolences. You should have said something. I would have called Kitty and told her to pay all your checks."

"Thank you," I mumbled, feeling the familiar prick of guilt. "It was bound to happen."

"What's next?" he asked, seeing the grim determination in my eyes.

"I'm going to be like Ramirez," I told him, referencing the old timer who sold me my first shop and operated purely on cash. "Cash for my supplies until I can pay off every vendor, including you for mechanic parts."

"Don't sweat me, Georgie," he said, a wave of his hand dismissing his own considerable stake.

"No, Sam. Put me on C.O.D. I want it that way. And don't buy any more insurance paper from Mike or me."

"Why?"

"I have a bad feeling. Humor me."

Sam rose, a big man with a bigger heart, and pulled me into a hug, kissing both my cheeks. "I'm here for you, son," he rumbled. "This will pass; stay positive."

* * *

That evening, Elena picked up Chinese takeout. We sat at the kitchen table, proper plates, an assortment of small white boxes open between us. I dipped an egg roll into plum sauce, while Elena finished her wonton soup, tilting the coffee cup to get every last drop. She set it down, her hands wrapped around the warmth.

"I have fifteen thousand in the bank, baby," she said, her voice soft but firm. "I can let you have it, and don't say no."

"No," I said, though my gut twisted with the need. "But thank you, truly, for the offer."

I scraped crumbs from my plate into the trash and started washing our dishes. She wiped down the table, packed away the leftovers. We converged on the couch, the television a low murmur. Two glasses of wine, not Canadian Club, sat half-full between us. We leaned in, our lips meeting in a gentle, slow kiss, savoring small sips.

"You know I'm not taking any of your money. But thank you. I thought you only had five thousand saved."

She smiled, a faint, sad curve of her lips. "David gave me five when I went to Hawaii, and another five when I met him in New York."

I chuckled, resisting the urge to make a comparison to Ava and Emma's burgeoning side business. "You're worth more," I said.

She sighed, a world of complicated emotion in the sound. "I know."

George Hatcher

* * *

The next morning, while Elena, Susie, and Alexa held down the fort on the shop floor, I was in my office with Carlos, my lawyer. I handed him a list: the check-cashing places holding bounced checks, three vendors whose checks had also cratered, and another list of everyone I owed for parts, places where I still had credit. Normally, my accountant would handle these at the end of the month. This month, there was no normal.

"You need to make a deal with the companies holding those checks," Carlos advised, his voice grave. "This could easily become criminal. The amounts aren't small."

"What do you suggest?"

"Give them as much cash as you can, and a promissory note. Promise to pay the amount owed plus interest within a set timeframe or in installments. If they accept the note and the cash, the matter becomes civil. If you fail to pay later, they can't go to the police for criminal charges."

"If I give them a note, I will pay them," I said, looking him dead in the eye. "Tell me again exactly what I have to do."

* * *

My first call was to Mike, to find out how many checks he had out that were being held.

"I owe fifteen thousand," Mike said, his voice unusually quiet. "I'm going to need payroll. And Sam just told me he's not buying any more paper for now. You forgot to tell me." He gave a short, humorless chuckle. He already knew everything—the bounced checks at my main shop, the groceries, the twenty dollars cash. He was completely up to date.

"I need to go around and get everyone holding checks to accept a promissory note from me. And I need to take cash with me, not just a note."

"What do you mean, a note?"

I explained. "A promissory note is like an IOU."

"Tell me what to do."

"Can you get me ten thousand from your guys?"

"I can, plus I need payroll."

"Do it," I urged. "And be ready for fireworks. You might get lucky for now, but the longer it takes, the deeper the hole. I'm in for over eighty thousand."

"It's okay," Mike said, a strange nonchalance in his tone. "Vicki and I have been thinking of splitting to her hometown in Springfield, Illinois." He chuckled again. "She can get a job like she has now. Says the cost of living is cheap compared to here. Fuck, I can take it easy."

I didn't plan to renew his lease when the first year was up, and that deadline was fast approaching.

* * *

My first stop was Mark's check-cashing place. I owed him twenty-five thousand. He had collected his "juice" for cashing and holding the checks, but that was petty cash compared to what he was out now. I met him in his fortified cash room, where two clerks worked behind thick glass, and a shotgun stood next to his desk. On his desk, within easy reach, was a handgun.

"Mark," I said, keeping my voice calm, "I have two thousand in cash. No receipt needed—call it interest, whatever you want. I'll give you a promissory note for the twenty-five thousand, payable in six months in one lump sum. I'll pay you a thousand a month until then, no matter what, and then the full balance will be due."

Mark was not happy. He reached over, his hand resting on his gun. "How are you going to pay me in six months if you don't have it now? What the fuck am I going to do with two thousand dollars? That ain't shit compared to what you owe me on these checks." He waved the stack of bounced checks two inches from my face.

"I'm shutting down the drains I have," I explained, forcing myself to ignore the gun. "I'm only keeping the main shop at Brooklyn and Rowan. It's a moneymaker. I'll pay you. If you sue me, my attorney says you'll eventually get your money, but it will take time. Will you at least think about it?"

"I'm so pissed at you," he repeated, his voice rising, his right hand moving from resting on the gun to picking it up, pointing it directly at me.

"You could do that," I said, looking him straight in the eye, refusing to flinch. "Then you'd never see the twenty-five thousand."

"I am so pissed at you," he said again, louder this time.

In his line of business, holdups were a risk, but the security of this room was ironclad. The look on his face was chilling, but more than fear, I felt a deep, burning embarrassment that it had come to this.

"Hey Mark, I'm here, humble as can be. I'm not afraid of the gun or the shotguns. I'm embarrassed I'm here under these circumstances. I apologize for letting you down."

My attorney had prepared typewritten promissory notes. All I needed was Mark's signature, acknowledging his agreement.

"Let me look at the note," he finally grunted.

I handed him the legal-sized envelope. He pulled out the note and read it, his brow furrowed. "There's no guarantee. No collateral. Nothing."

"It's my promise to pay you," I said. "Until now, I always came through. I never failed you. You never got a bounced check."

"What good is that if I end up with these no-good checks?" He picked up the checks and waved them in front of my face again. In any other situation, I might have lost my temper. But not now. I owed this man. I had nothing to show for the cash I'd taken from him to pay shop bills—my car and Elena's car were paid for with Vegas winnings.

His eyebrows bunched further, a deep frown settling. "Hey, you high or something?"

"You've got to be kidding," I said, a dry laugh escaping me. "I was just thinking how fucked up this must be for you."

"Where's the two Gs?"

I took out a pre-counted wad of bills, not all hundreds, and handed it to him. He put the gun down, though he still kept the barrel pointed in my direction.

"You can't give me more?"

"In one month, I'll be back with a thousand," I said.

Ten minutes later, I walked out with a signed copy of the note. Mark had signed, agreeing to the terms and conditions I had outlined.

Back at the shop, I wasn't sure I could stomach immediately facing another check-cashing proprietor. As I drove up, I knew something was wrong. The lights were out. Elena dashed out of the building, reaching my car window before I'd even stopped or opened the door.

"Water & Power shut off the lights, and the water," she blurted out, her voice tight with panic. "Their check bounced."

Kitty at the bank. That bitch.

"The guy who came out said to take the payment to their office. There's a five-hundred-dollar deposit needed in addition to the check amount."

I looked at the bill, a blur of numbers and addresses. "I don't even know where this is."

"We can't paint cars," Elena said, her voice strained. "Everything is out, baby."

"Blame it on the system," I muttered, shoving the bill into my pocket. "I'll rush over and pay. Be back ASAP."

I drove a mile to a field office, where I had to stand in line. By the time I finally reached the counter, it was already two-thirty. A dark-haired woman in a brown dress, perpetually frowning, accepted my cash and identification. She moved with the slow, deliberate grace of a sloth, speaking even slower. She adjusted her glasses, filled out a form, then delivered the blow.

"I'm afraid we can't turn everything back on for at least three hours."

I wanted to curse, to rage, but it wasn't her fault. I thanked her and left, feeling like I was drowning. Not figuratively—literally. Underwater and sinking fast. In the car, a manic, humorless laugh escaped me. What else could happen? What else could I do? A song about love on the radio grated on my ears. I turned it off. I couldn't handle music.

When I returned to the shop, I heard the reassuring hum of the exhaust fan and saw the glow of the oven lights. The overhead lights were still out, but the skylights let in enough daylight. Elena was already with a customer.

Then I saw Mauro, my electrician friend, who had wired the entire shop when I first opened. While I was at the utility company, he'd performed some electrical magic, hot-wiring power from the adjacent meat market. Wires snaked across the floor, feeding the spray booth, oven, and compressor. The moneymaker was running.

By the time Water & Power eventually showed up to fully restore everything, the last car was already in the oven. Thanks to Mauro, there had been minimal downtime. We got all the promised cars out that day.

That evening, as I locked up, Elena, Susie, Alexa, and I huddled in front of the gates. To say I was feeling emotional would be an understatement.

"I love you all," I said, my voice thick. "It won't always be like this. I promise."

Susie and Alexa left. Elena and I clung to each other in front of the Brooklyn entrance of Eastland Auto Center, exhausted. It had been the longest business day of my life, like running a marathon uphill. But Elena had been there, standing by.

Before heading home, we stopped to see Jesse and Chris. They were near closing, so I hugged them both, thanking them for Mauro's improvised electrical hookup. I'd already paid them for the groceries they'd packed for my team. They didn't probe about the power outage or what was truly going on.

* * *

The next morning, I braced myself for another check-cashing visit. This time, it was Icebox Moreno's shop, just opening for the day. Moreno wasn't his real name, but it fit—a massive ex-football player who'd lost his front teeth to an old tackle. He was in his thirties, his muscles having long since turned to fat, but he carried a chip on his shoulder and an obnoxious way of speaking, full of college football stories despite never graduating or going pro.

"I owe you fifteen thousand," I stated, cutting straight to it. "I don't have the money to pay it off right now, but I will."

I stood inside Moreno's fortified cash room. Money was everywhere, stacked behind two money counters. Even banks didn't display their cash like this.

"Mark called me yesterday and told me you gave him a note," Moreno growled, his voice thick. "I don't want a note. I prefer putting your ass in jail. You've got until tomorrow to bring me the cash."

"My lawyer said you have to prove intent," I countered, keeping my gaze steady. "I never intended this to happen. I can show you've cashed at least thirty of my checks. You got your juice, and none of those checks bounced. I doubt Mark suggested you file charges because if I go to jail, who's going to pay Mark?"

Moreno, maybe ten years my senior, was strange, but he'd always given me what I wanted in the past.

"I'll give you three months, but not six. It's only fifteen thousand."

"It's only thirteen thousand," I corrected. "Because I have two to give you now."

"I should send a friend to see you when you're sleeping."

I took a slow, silent breath. "That wouldn't be a good idea, Moreno. I have the same kind of friends. The difference is if I call for a favor, I don't have to pay. If you hire someone, you have to pay. Please don't push me. I'm here just as I went to Mark, apologetic and humble. I fucked up. My banker let me down."

Moreno finally smiled, a wide, unsettling grin that revealed his remaining teeth, some natural, some gold-plated replacements. "Let me look at the note."

He walked me to the door. I left with my signed copy of the promissory note and agreement. He kept the original and the two thousand dollars. He had agreed to the six-month plan, just like Mark.

"I'll see you in thirty days with my first payment," I said.

He simply nodded and patted my back. "You got the kind of friends that make house calls?" he asked, a glint in his eye.

I didn't turn around, just said, "Yes."

* * *

I had one more check-cashing company to visit, but I decided to call and arrange it for the morning. I went back to the shop, relieved to see the lights on, the hum of business restored. I'd never forget the day I spent driving around, desperately trying to cover my ass.

I kissed Elena in passing as I headed up to my office. "How did you do?" she asked.

I turned and gave her a thumbs-up, no need to burden her with the particulars of Moreno's veiled threats. On my desk, Elena's neat handwriting had replaced my frantic charts of checks.

Kathy called. She said it was personal. You have the phone number.

I fought the urge to call her immediately, but before the afternoon was over, I dialed.

"I didn't think you'd ever call. That's why I called you."

"Hey, I'm glad you did. How are you?"

"I'm good. I could be better if we met up."

When I'd worked with Matt, I could disappear without worrying about the shop or the employees who depended on me. But who was I kidding? I was the boss now, I made my own hours.

"Tell me where and when, and I'll get away," I said.

George Hatcher

* * *

Elena drove us home in her car that evening. We hadn't decided on dinner, so she pulled into traffic and asked, "Did you get the message?"

"Message?"

"From Kathy. I left it on your desk. Did you return the call?" Elena was watching traffic more than me, pulling into the right lane where restaurants lined the street.

"I did. I met her when I went to P.J.'s while you were away. She's married and has two friends who are married, too. We're just friends."

"Baby, you met her at P.J.'s, and now she's just a married friend? Married like Molly? Is this a new phase?"

I reached over to touch her face as she drove. I hadn't been to the tavern since before my son passed. Molly probably thought I'd died. If she cared, she would have come to the shop, it was right next door.

"Hello, are you still here?" Elena asked, a playful edge to her voice.

I laughed a little. "Baby, you and me, we're nutty. It's not just me."

"Give me back your hand," she said, taking it, kissing my palm, then the tips of my fingers, just like she always did. I reached down, my hand finding her through her jeans.

There was always something missing when I was with Susie, Alexa, Ava, or Emma. But sex between Elena and me was perfect. Elena was the complete package.

"Baby, I've got to 'spring' this afternoon," I told Elena the next morning at work, using her word.

"Are you coming back soon?"

"Not *your* kind of spring away. I'll be back this afternoon."

"You're not heading for Vegas?"

I shook my head. "After I saw Mark, I was ready to head out. No, I'm not going to Vegas." I kissed her. "And I have to see First Street Check Cashing."

"Hope you can get this one to take the note this morning. Then you only have three vendors who have checks. They should be easier, huh?"

"I'm heartbroken that I'm where I am."

She placed her palms on my cheeks, and we kissed. "You'll feel better when you spring."

The third check-casher, Lalo, was Mexican. He reminded me of Lion and Tigre, though I doubted he had the backing of someone as powerful as their grandmother. He wasn't easy with the terms of the note, but he neither threatened the police nor violence. What he *did* propose was a curse, one that would last until I paid him. I owed him fifteen thousand. It took almost two hours of negotiation, but when I left, he had accepted the two thousand in cash and the promissory note. I didn't even have to invoke Lion and Tigre.

* * *

I drove out to the San Fernando Valley and met Kathy. By the time I arrived, she had already rented the room and was waiting in the hotel lobby. An eerie déjà vu washed over me, a fleeting recall of Christine, of meeting in a hotel room. This hotel was different, and Kathy was nothing like Christine, but there was something about the clandestine nature of a rented room that felt the same, even though neither of us was particularly sneaking. We went up to the room and undressed quickly.

"What time do you have to be home?" I asked.

"Tomorrow morning, around nine will do."

"I didn't bring clothes," I said.

"Good. You don't need clothes," she replied, her eyes sparkling. "Come, do like last time. Make each other feel good."

Kathy hit the bed, beckoning me with her hands.

Pages of Passion Book 4: Threads of Destiny

Kathy

* * *

I was back at the shop before closing. At the foot of the stairs, I paused and gestured to Elena. "C'mon."

She followed me up to my office. I sat at my desk, sifting through the accumulated mail.

"How did you do with Lalo this morning?" she asked.

"He finally accepted, but there may be consequences."

Elena's face paled, and she wrung her hands. "What kind of consequences?"

"If I don't pay him, he's going to put a curse on me, and I don't think he's joking."

She looked a little less anxious then, letting out a tiny bark of laughter. I was probably more suspicious of Mexican curses than she was. I'm not saying I believe in them, and I'm not saying I don't. It's just better not to have that kind of ill will floating around.

"I didn't think you'd be back this soon. You don't need to tell me."

"Yeah, I saw her," I admitted.

"You feel better?"

I took a silent, slow breath before exhaling. "I do things with my eyes open, and then I wonder why I did it."

"You mean today?"

"Not just today."

She came around my desk and settled onto my lap, hugging me, her cheek against mine. "I can't say I'm sorry."

"G, it's okay. We have an understanding. It's fine. Strange is okay."

"Is that why you 'spring' to the Texan? That's no longer strange. Or is it?"

She nuzzled and sniffed the nape of my neck, her fingers touching my slightly damp hair. "Did you shower?"

"Gross," I teased.

And she used my own word. "Yeah, right, gross." We laughed, the tension momentarily broken.

"Is she pretty?" she asked.

"I never told you she was pretty."

"On the phone, she sounded pretty. Baby, come on, tell me. You know you want to. Spill."

"Tell me about the Texan, and I'll tell you anything you want to know."

"Here and now or at home?"

I glanced at the wall clock. "Let's shut it down and go home. I want to hear."

* * *

The next morning, Sergeant Lass from the Sheriff's Department, East Los Angeles Office, called.

"Hatcher, I have two complaints about insufficient funds to present to the district attorney. One from Atlantic Ford, a check for eleven hundred, and one from Atlantic Dodge, a check for eight hundred."

"Sergeant," I said, trying to sound calm, "I have the cash and planned on visiting them today to take care of this. I'm sorry it happened. It's a misunderstanding with my banker."

"Listen, Hatcher, we are the Sheriff's Department. We aren't a collection agency, but we do jail persons who issue bad checks. You understand that?"

"Loud and clear, sir."

I heard a cough on his end, picturing a big man behind a desk. I'd lived with all kinds of cops—in the brig, LA County Jail, DVI, even Tijuana cops. Cops didn't scare me. I didn't want to end up in jail, but I wasn't intimidated by a grumpy cop like Sergeant Lass. Less than an hour later, I had paid off both checks and their associated bank fees, returning to the shop with the cancelled checks in hand.

"Good work, G. Now you only have the creditors you won't pay this month."

"Yeah, but I have to pay these three check-cashers. I gave them notes for a thousand a month each, and six months from now, I have to come up with the balance."

"I don't believe you're sweating what happens in six months. Am I right?"

We looked at each other, eye to eye. He was right. I wasn't sweating. "I'm not worried."

I had some insurance checks coming to me, but most of those went to Sam. The total was small at best. The rest of the receivables from insurance companies for Mike's shop belonged to Sam now. When the check arrived, it went straight to him. I couldn't count on that money, and that was okay. I was tired of debt. It was time to face the music. I'd find a way.

Without Chester and the other three check-cashers who I had given promissory notes, I no longer had a spot to float a check, use the money, and cover it later. The check-cashers had been my bank for Vegas. Unless I found new ones—and I didn't plan to—that source was gone. The shop I kept calling Mike's was still technically mine; he owned one-third of the profits, *if* there were any. That meant the financial holes he was digging by cashing checks would soon impact me. I knew it.

* * *

Elena knew many of the insurance adjusters who frequented our shop.

"Baby, I need you to do some dirty work for me. Can you do me a favor?"

"You got it. What do you need?"

"Call the key people who send business to this location. Have them send it to Whittier. Mike can handle it until we implode."

Elena let out a shrill whistle that cut through my eardrums. "With pleasure," she said, a grim satisfaction in her tone.

"It's still my shop, baby. I want the pressure off this place. This one has to survive."

I called Mike and told him I'd be sending him two body men as soon as they finished their current jobs, and to expect a surge in business.

"How do I handle it?" he asked, the usual calm in his voice.

"Best way you can. I've got your back. It's on me, brother."

Mike was always so calm, so cool; it was hard to believe he had once beaten a man to death in a rage, only avoiding prison by being committed to the youth authority.

* * *

My accountant still came over, but only to do the monthly sales invoices. After he prepared the final payroll reports for the IRS and California, I restructured everyone as outside service contractors, eliminating formal payroll. Ramirez's voice, from ages ago, echoed in my ear telling me to do exactly that, and I had ignored him. My CPA warned it would catch up to me. I figured what would catch up to me were the sales tax and payroll taxes I hadn't paid, and a year of income tax for both corporations and myself personally. I was royally screwed, but I was taking it a day at a time.

Without insurance work at the main shop, I didn't have to worry about buying parts there. Mike, however, had that worry. He still had some credit, as his was a different corporation, even if some vendors were the same ones who'd cut me off. Mike made it work, just as I would have if he hadn't been there.

When paint was delivered to my shop, Elena paid the invoice in cash. If the mechanic needed parts, which was often several times a day, we bought them from Eagle Parts, Sam's company, paying cash. The money coming in from painting, minor bodywork, and mechanic work was squirreled away to pay for everything, including payroll.

The upholstery department was on their own now. I couldn't bail them out anymore. I had made it clear to the brothers: they paid four hundred a week for their space and use of my sewing machines, keeping all their income. I only wanted my four hundred a week. No more math headaches.

From all appearances, we were doing okay. No one could tell we were running short of cash, except those I owed money to. They didn't bad-mouth me too badly; I still ordered from them and paid cash on delivery. I kept assuring them I would pay the past-due balances and that I was no Ramirez.

"Ramirez wasn't doing one-fifth the business I'm giving you," I'd tell those who brought him up.

I hated the position I was in. My credit had gone into the toilet almost overnight.

I still had to deal with Graham at Bank of America, but since I didn't write any checks from there, I only heard from him if I was late on my equipment loans. I had an equipment loan with Kitty and a ten-thousand-dollar line of credit that I had maxed out. I purposely avoided her calls. I held back making payments on the loans for two reasons: I didn't have enough money, and I hated her for starting the falling dominoes when she bounced all my checks. I was sure the only reason she hadn't come after me legally was because of Sam. Mike still banked with her, but he was fucking her as needed. It was ironic, because the account Mike had at her bank was *my* account—I was the president of that corporation. But I didn't want to stir up dust and get Mike shut down. Whatever favor she extended to Mike ultimately benefited me. She had to know that.

Mike gave me unwanted advice on handling Kitty, but I ignored it. That was one cat I wasn't taking on.

"I'm sure you can get what you need from Kitty," Mike pressed. "Just take her to lunch. She asks about you all the time. She says she's sorry she didn't go the extra mile for you. She didn't know Leonie had died, and that's why you weren't—"

"Brother, man," I interrupted, my voice sharp. "I would not fuck Kitty with your dick, much less mine. Got it?"

I heard the door to my office open and close as Elena walked in, catching that last line of conversation. A snort of laughter escaped her.

"I hear you loud and clear, brother," Mike said, a hint of amusement in his tone.

"Interesting," Elena said, then burst into peals of laughter, collapsing onto the couch. "Would you fuck me with Mike's dick?"

"Gross," I said, though I couldn't help but smile.

"Not gross," she retorted, still laughing.

Sometimes, I truly wondered about Elena. She was as warped as I was.

* * *

My office window offered a view of the parking lot, part of Safeway's lot, the two shop entrances, and most of the shop floor. The girls were in the small office, once Ramirez's, next to the customer waiting room. It was that lull in the afternoon before the five o'clock rush.

I saw a white Pinto in the lot. For a moment, my mind flashed to Olivia, the Shakey's Pizza waitress I'd lost touch with. But it wasn't Olivia. The woman driving was a blonde. It was Molly.

I double-timed it down the stairs and across the shop floor, reaching the Brooklyn entrance just as she walked up. She saw me and smiled, that mesmerizing smile.

"Molly, I miss you," I said, straight off, unable to filter it.

She gave me a look of disbelief. "If that were true, you'd come see me like before."

I had never hugged or kissed her before, but that changed as she kissed my cheek. I caught a faint, sweet whiff of her fragrance.

"What a pleasant surprise," I managed.

"I'd like to paint my car."

"Want to see some colors?"

"Any color but white," she said. "You pick it out for me."

"Seriously?"

"Please do it for me. How much?"

"One dollar," I said.

"What's the catch?"

"No catch," I promised.

"Your sign says thirty-five dollars. That's a good price."

"When do you want to drop it off?"

"Now. I'll get a ride home when I get off."

I checked my watch. She started work at four. "Your car will be ready tomorrow. Is that okay?"

"Fine. Take your time. I can do without it for a couple of days."

"No need. It will be ready at this time tomorrow."

"Great. Want me to sign anything?"

"Nope. Want me to walk you to the tavern?"

"I know the way, but I'd like the company. I still have fifteen minutes."

I wanted to take her up to my office, to hold her, to kiss her properly. Instead, I walked her to the tavern, talking all the way there. Then I came back.

Elena stood at the open door, watching me cross the street and approach the shop. As I got closer, she smiled, but there was a knowing glint in her eyes.

"I won't compete with her," she said.

I was puzzled. "What do you mean?"

"Just what I said." She kissed me then turned, walking towards an arriving customer.

I drove Molly's Pinto inside and told the sander to send Luis to me when he finished the car he was painting—the last of the day. Susie asked if I needed an invoice for the Pinto. Then Alexa asked. Then Elena.

"No invoice," I said.

"All cars are supposed to have an invoice," Elena insisted, her voice flat.

I laughed, but Elena didn't.

"Okay, write an invoice. Put Molly for the name. I don't even know her last name."

"What are we doing to it?"

"Minor bodywork as needed, and pick a color other than white."

I should have never said that. Elena had the car painted yellow, a bright taxi-cab yellow.

"How could you do that?" I demanded, staring at the garish vehicle.

"Baby, it's like new, beautiful! She's going to love it. Watch." Elena was all smiles, her victory evident.

When Molly arrived the next evening to pick up the car, I was already looking out for her.

"I took out all the little dents and scratches," I explained, "but I let Elena pick out the color, and she picked yellow. Please, leave it another day, and I'll repaint it."

Molly looked at the car, then burst into laughter. "It's cute! Leave it. It's okay."

"You have to love it, and I know you don't love it," I pressed, feeling a stubborn streak.

"It's okay, George. If I hate it later, I promise I'll tell you. I'm not shy."

The car *did* look cute, but I wasn't going to agree. Elena had been deliberately mean, and she knew it. I imagined the fucking Texan bringing over his Rolls Royce and what I'd do to *his* car.

Molly took out her wallet, insisting on paying.

"Give me a dollar," I said.

"Please, George."

She handed me a dollar and kissed both my cheeks. "Did you get the divorce yet?"

She stood there, car door open, in the noisy shop, waiting for my answer. We were the focus of all eyes, especially Elena's, but I wouldn't look around to acknowledge it. She was still waiting.

"Not yet. I'm pushing it now," I said. "I haven't been over because I have business issues. And my baby boy died."

I should not have said that.

The expectation drained from her face, replaced by profound sympathy. I saw a tender, sad look in her eyes, but mostly, I felt uncomfortable for bringing it up. Molly closed her car door, her fingertips lightly grazing my forearm.

"I'm so sorry," she said.

I took a deep breath. "I'm sorry I told you," I managed, forcing a smile. The life of my son was an immeasurable loss. He was not an excuse.

She hugged me right there, holding me close. "What do you mean?"

"I'm good now," I said, pulling back. "It's been a few months."

She opened the car door again. "Are you going out at all? Or is it too soon for you?"

"I'm good now," I repeated.

"There's a boat cruise in San Pedro two weeks from Saturday night. I have tickets. I'm going with girlfriends. Can you come?"

I stared at her, mesmerized by her smile, so unique and captivating. "How about your husband?"

"He comes to the tavern when I leave at eight, and Adrian starts work." I thought about Adrian, who adored Molly's husband.

"Sure. I'll buy a ticket or two."

"I have a ticket for you. Come to the tavern today or tomorrow, and I'll give it to you. I don't have it with me now."

"Thanks, Molly."

She blew me a kiss and drove off. I stood watching until her yellow Pinto disappeared from view, then turned to the front entrance of the shop, catching Elena's gaze. I walked up to her.

"I told you she'd love it," Elena said, a smirk playing on her lips.

"Elena, I'm surprised. Why pull a stunt like that?"

"Get serious. It wasn't a stunt. We have yellow right there." She pointed to the color samples on display.

"It was a cheap shot," I said, and walked up to my office, the memory of Molly's smile, and Elena's calculating one, warring in my head.

Author's Notes:

1 When I married my first wife, I went AWOL from the Navy and settled in Juarez, Mexico, her hometown. She had two friends named Lion and Tigre who were the nephews of a very powerful cartel head.

2 Ramirez sold me my first shop. He had been there for years and was on the way to being evicted when I came along and made a deal with him.

Chapter 18
Running On Fumes

The cash cow's lifeblood lived in my office safe. We kept cash here from the sales at the car wash shop, Soto Street, and the main shop. All of us-I and all my employees-were sustained by the money in this safe. I counted two thousand in twenties and put it in my pocket where it joined three hundred and change. By the time I got to my car, I felt guilty. Like I had taken it from a piggy bank.

I was wearing a stylish three-quarter length Alpaca jacket that Alicia had insisted I get for myself. The locker drama seemed like a distant memory, almost like a dream, but the Alpaca jacket was real and warm. I said nothing to anyone. I went straight to my car and headed for Las Vegas. Elena would be stranded at the office; her car was at the apartment. She wouldn't really be stranded, but she'd have to get a taxi or have Alexa drive her. Fuck it. I didn't want to think about the details. Thinking was not involved.

Four hours later, I finally pulled into the self-park of the Dunes Hotel in Las Vegas. The brisk winter air hit me as I stepped out of the car; Vegas is painfully cold in winter and scorching hot in summer. As I walked toward the nearest entrance to the bustling casino, the distant sounds of laughter and clinking chips set the atmosphere, intensifying my anticipation.

I went straight to the cashier, handing over my twenties in exchange for twenty crisp hundred-dollar bills.

Finding a table that resonated with the right energy, I took a seat. The dealer was a young woman named Lucy, her hair pulled back tightly, a determined look in her sharp eyes. As I sat down, I paused to reflect: was I afraid to lose the money I had come with? It felt heavy in my pocket, a tangible reminder of the risk.

Looking back now, my biggest wins in Las Vegas came when I placed bold cash bets. The thrill surged through me as I declared, "Money plays." I set the two thousand dollars on the table. Lucy counted the bills, her lips curving into a smile as she said, "Money plays. Two thousand." The pit boss, a steady presence, smiled knowingly at me though I was certain I had never seen him before. "Money plays," he echoed before strolling away.

The table held four other players, the tension palpable. Halfway through the game, Lucy shuffled the deck, and I felt the cool breeze from the air conditioning on my skin. I slipped my face-down card into the mix with a sense of eagerness. I had two face cards, while Lucy showed a three. I didn't have enough to double down; all I could do was ride the hand. I knew I would win—I was a positive thinker, after all. And I did win. The dealer paid me in colorful chips, which remained on the table, a testament to my success.

After the tumultuous days I had been through, the two thousand I had just won felt like a fortune.

A waitress approached for drink orders; her voice was warm and familiar, reminiscent of Donna. "Are you on water or something else, sweetie?" she asked, her smile brightening the moment.

"Water, please," I replied, the simplicity comforting amidst the excitement.

"Money plays," I said to Lucy. I had two thousand in cash and the two thousand in chips I had just won—a total of four thousand on the table.

Lucy busted. Now, the stakes climbed higher: I had two thousand cash plus six thousand in chips on the table. "Money plays," I repeated, the phrase feeling like a mantra.

I sensed a crowd gathering, but my focus remained on Lucy. I pushed forward with confidence; she dealt the cards, and luck seemed to be on my side. Lucy busted.

"Can we change color?" Lucy asked.

"Sure," I replied.

Lucy changed my hundred-dollar chips to five-hundred-dollar chips. I put the green cash in my pocket and let the chips ride, feeling the eyes of the crowd behind me.

"One more time, Lucy, money plays."

"Money plays," she echoed.

Yet, anxiety flickered at the edges of my mind. I was starting to worry about losses—I couldn't afford to play that way. The dealer revealed a deuce. I took the two thousand cash out of my pocket and placed it with my chips. "Double down, two thousand," I said.

Lucy counted the cash. "Money plays," she called out.

I don't remember if the pit boss circled back or not.

Lucy busted again. Overwhelmed with a rush of victory, I handed her a five hundred dollar chip, slipped my two thousand back into my pocket, and collected all my wonderful five hundred dollar chips, putting them in my pockets.

As I walked away, my heart raced—I'd turned that initial investment into thirty thousand dollars, minus the five hundred I gave Lucy. I remember feeling the thrill of victory echoing through the casino's vibrant atmosphere. I knew I wasn't done playing, but I was done playing at that table—or maybe for that night. I had to shake off the worry about losing.

In the car, I took the two thousand I had come with and put it in an inner jacket pocket that had a zipper. "I'm not touching this," I said aloud to myself.

My other pocket held twenty-nine thousand four hundred dollars—my winnings minus the hundred I gave to the cashier when I cashed my chips in.

I could go home a winner.

I drove to the Tropicana. I wondered if Donna would be in the bar tonight. I went into the casino and never stopped at the bar. The whole place was packed. The blackjack tables were packed. I walked around, waiting for a seat, checking the heat or chill of the tables by stopping for a few minutes. I walked to the bar and looked around. Donna was not there.

I walked back to the action. I picked a table. The dealer was Elena. She looked nothing like my Elena, but that was a lucky name for me. I never liked the middle seat, but I liked the dealer. I liked the name. Her badge didn't say where she was from. I introduced myself.

I took two thousand and played it on my firsthand. I had thirteen. The dealer was showing fourteen. Damn. I hit my thirteen and got an eight. The dealer hit fourteen and went bust.

I didn't take my money off the table.

"Play the chips and cash," I said to the dealer.

"Money plays."

The pit boss didn't bother to come by from wherever he was. He repeated. I won four thousand. I got smiles from both sides of me. Elena was cute and cuter when she smiled at the hundred-dollar tip I gave her.

I put the green in my jacket pocket where it came from and played all my chips. In ten minutes, I had twelve thousand in chips in front of me.

"Elena, play all this."

I got the oohs and aaas. The crowd started gathering. I drank some water. The smart side of my brain told me to slow down. What's the rush?

I betrayed some excitement when I won.

"Can I get five hundred chips?" I asked Elena. I gave Elena another hundred.

A little later, a host recognized me. "You didn't call me," she said.

My eyes were on the table. I said, "I want to stay."

"Have me paged. I got you covered," the host said.

Hours later, Elena had taken two breaks. I had been up and down. Instead of leaving all my chips on the table, I pulled and pocketed as I continued to play. I had twenty thousand in five-hundred-dollar chips and a couple thousand in hundreds in front of me. I was getting tired and hungry.

I played twenty thousand.

"Elena, I'm walking win or lose." She nodded.

I could feel the anxiety of the others at my table. If I looked behind me, I'd see the lookers who amble around looking. Looking back on my age and look, I wonder what the lookers wondered about me, like who is this kid, maybe he sells marijuana.

Elena busted. I had twelve and stayed.

"If it was legal, I'd kiss you," I said to Elena. My fellow players clapped as she paid me with five-hundred-dollar chips. I didn't want any thousand chips. I'd learned my lesson. I gave Elena two hundred dollars. She made a thousand off me in tips, but that was my whistle. I wanted to scream and whoop and whistle. I never learned how to whistle like Elena, so tipping would have to do. The waitress came by as I was pocketing my chips. I gave her a hundred dollars. At the cashier, I just took a chance and unloaded everything I had in chips. I figured I had won seventy thousand plus, but I had played a long time and lost count. The cashier paid me eighty-seven thousand dollars. She didn't ask for ID or anything. I gave her a hundred. She beamed. I turned around, and there was my pretty little straight-haired hostess with a room key. Long straight hair, silky, brunette. She had an Italian look and a wide smile.

"What else do you want?" she said. "Anything."

"This will do for now, but don't be surprised if I have you paged." I gave her two hundred.

"You're so generous, George."

I kissed her cheek and walked towards the bar. My jacket pockets carried my money much better than my jeans pockets. I took a seat.

There was live entertainment. A guy was singing and wiggling to the Twist. The crowd was twisting along with him. It was crowded and a riot of color and movement. I was looking for Donna, still. The song switched to Rick Nelson singing about some teenage broken heart. The dancing got a little less frantic. I was seated on a barstool when I saw thought I saw her Marilyn Monroe hair. I saw her on another stool by the bar. It was reason enough to get up and walk over. I got close to make sure it was Donna, and she turned around. She blinked, and my image must have registered.

"G, it's you."

She was off that stool and on her feet. We hugged. She picked up her coat from the empty seat next to her, and we headed up to my suite.

"You look great," I said.

"I bought a lot of nice clothes with some of the money you gave me the last time. I owe you so much, G."

I took her hand as we walked. "You owe me nothing," I said. "I'm starved, are you?"

"I can eat," she said. "Are you ordering a big steak for yourself?" she giggled.

"I am, and one for you."

"No, not a steak."

We laughed as the elevator took us up to the penthouse.

Donna didn't ask how much I'd won or even if I won. Either she didn't care, or someone had told her not to ask that question of a client. Fuck, I didn't want to think that I was only a client to Donna. I liked her too much. I liked Ava and Emma, too.

Imagine a huge apartment with two bedrooms, three bathrooms, a living room, a dining room, and a den, and even the bathrooms, with floor to ceiling windows. I'd never been to the suite before. It was stocked with the wines I liked so much.

While Donna filled the tub for herself, I showered in the other bathroom and again realized I had no change of clothes. It was too late to hit the mall. I dried off and put on the fancy terry robe, and went to the living room desk to order room service. I knocked on the bathroom door and found she was under a thousand bubbles.

"You dig bubble baths?"

"I love these monster tubs."

"Take your time. I'm going to order. Tell me what you want to eat."

"A hamburger, no fries, a salad instead. We'll drink wine, yes?"

"Yes," I said.

I called room service and ordered. Then I asked the operator to connect me to a Los Angeles number. I called my apartment. Elena didn't answer. She was a light sleeper. She must not have gone to my apartment. It was too late to call her aunt's house. It was almost one. I turned off the worry about there being no answer back home and where Elena was. I was sure she was safe and okay. I figured my fish could fast for one day. I would deal with that tomorrow.

I was ravenous, but all I needed was a steak the size of a Volkswagen. Other than that, we didn't eat or drink much, but we did have a lot of sex. At one point, Donna said something she'd never said before.

"Not so hard, G. I love it – you're a monster tonight." She tempered that because she was giggling when she said it.

The phone rang and woke me up. Donna didn't even stir. It was nine. It had to be morning. I couldn't tell because the room door and the blackout drapes were shut tight.

I reached for the phone next to the illuminated bedside clock.

"Yes."

"I took a chance you'd be there," Elena said.

"I called you, but no one answered."

"I stayed at my aunt's."

"Are you okay?"

"The question is if are you okay."

Donna stirred.

"I'm good. I had to get away. I did good. I'll call you back."

"I only wanted to make sure you're alright."

"Thanks," I said. I thought of the yellow car.

I lay back down. I don't know why I felt like someone had beat me up. I certainly didn't have a hangover. I spooned Donna, kissed the back of her neck, and passed out.

I gave Donna a thousand dollars.

"You don't have to pay me any longer," she said. "We're friends."

"I hope I always have the money to pay you," I said.

She saw it was a thousand and tried to give it back. "Two hundred works, G, or nothing works too."

At four in the afternoon, I checked out of the hotel. Donna was in my car. I drove less than a mile off the strip and dropped her off at the Desert Motel where she lived, a compound composed of a long, skinny, squat building with a low flat roof, and beside it, a double-stack of the same style of sand-colored building. The motel's name was written in white lights on a dark green sign with two neon cactuses planted in a triangular patch of thirsty-looking grass and shrubs. It was daylight, so the sign was off. I didn't go in to check out the reception desk, but I saw where it was through the doors just beyond a low concrete awning stretching across two lanes of the parking lot.

"Are you good here?"

"I am. It's clean. I get fresh bedding every two days. I have no utilities. It's not the Taj Mahal, but the front desk takes messages when I get a call. Motel living at its finest. I get all the perks."

We got out of the car, but I left my motor running. I gave her a bear hug.

"I don't do any business here. We can come here and hang out if you happen to be down and out." She kissed me.

"Let's hope I'm never down and out, but I thank you. You're beautiful, Donna."

She sighed.

"So are you."

Chapter 19
Back From Vegas A Winner

I got to my apartment just after nine that night. Elena was not there. I put the cash in five white athletic socks and put them under my mattress.

I called Elena at her aunt's house.

"I noticed you got your car but didn't stay."

"I got it yesterday," she said. "I don't want to be there if you aren't there."

"I'm back," I said. "Am I jogging alone tomorrow, or are you coming over?"

She was silent.

"If you promise to shower before I get there."

I laughed.

"Gross."

"Gross my ass," she said. "I have a blonde named Molly here to contend with and another blonde named Donna in Las Vegas."

"Baby, contend is too extreme."

"If there is nothing between us, then I agree, contend is extreme."

In the long silence, I heard her breathing. I practiced my calm breathing. Two breaths. Three.

"You never been jealous before," I said. "How about springing to the Texan?"

I heard a sigh.

"I'm coming over, but we are not fucking tonight."

"Hurry," I said. "I'm too tired to fuck anyway."

She actually growled into the phone. "I'm going to choke you."

I showered. When Elena arrived, I hugged her. She didn't choke me as promised. She pounded my chest, not hard, a gesture demonstrating how bothered she was. My guess is that her concern wasn't Donna. It was Molly.

Elena never asked me if I was still a winner or how much.

* * *

In the morning, Elena and I jogged together. As cool as I was being, I was still full of the win, and the run jostled the news right out of me before we'd finished the first block.

"I won, baby," I said.

"I figured. That's what you said on the phone. But then you didn't come back. You stayed another day with Donna. I wasn't sure if you hit the tables again, and it went the other way."

"No way. I don't go back."

"I'm happy for you, baby," she turned. I turned to watch her. We were running shoulder to shoulder, probably should have been looking ahead, but as luck would have it, neither of us fell on our asses.

"You're beautiful, Elena."

"You never call me by my name. Why now?"

"Elena, Elena, Elena."

We stopped. I hugged her. We'd just started jogging, so we weren't warmed up yet. The weather was cold. I kissed her, and she responded. Our teeth rubbed. I put my hands on her face, and we pressed together, lip to lip. In the middle of a street, I felt her hand down there on me.

"Let's skip jogging today," I said. "I can think of alternative exercise. I'm up for it."

"Yeah, you are," she said, checking for herself. "Let's."

We ran back to the apartment and never made it to the bed. We hit the living room floor, wrestled out of our joggers. Our bodies came together like when I used to weld metal to metal. Our bodies bonded for a long time, changing like a kaleidoscope, stirring, her on top, rolling, me on top, we did it all. Her short hair was still a turn-on for me, a bonfire. She had always played with my curly hair. I couldn't keep my hands off her pixie. Afterward, while we were both naked and lying on the carpeted floor, I reached for the phone. Elena was lying perpendicular to me, her head on my stomach. I called Alexa, told her we were running late, and asked her to pick up Susie and open up without us, then called Susie to confirm, saving her the usual streetcar ride.

It didn't take long for winter to convince us to put our robes and warm slippers on. Elena started the coffee, started warming some pan dulce, and sat down at the kitchen table.

"I'll be right back," I said.

I returned to the kitchen and put the socks between us on the table.

"Are those socks dirty?" She stood up like they were nuclear.

I put my hand on her shoulder and coaxed her back down in her seat.

"Those socks are brand new, never been worn, and stuffed with the proceeds from Vegas."

Elena exploded with laughter. She squeezed one of the socks, getting a feel for what stuffed meant, then shook off my hand and started jumping up and down. I got excited and started jumping up and down right along with her. I was still full of the win, and I don't know how I'd kept my calm anyway. Good thing I lived on the first floor with the parking under me.

"I'm not going to play the fireman again," I said after coming back down to earth. "I'm not going to pay past-due bills. I'm already fucked. My credit is fucked. I have to give the three check cashers a thousand a month no matter what. When I do that, it's going to come from Eastland One. I'm dumping the car wash and Soto Street."

"Good for you," Elena said, excited. "When? And what about the employees?"

"I'll give them severance pay. As soon as Soldado finishes the Impala he's restoring, I'm out of that, too."

Elena took the pan dulce out of the oven and put them on a plate beside the socks before she warmed up my coffee and sat down.

"Are you okay with this? This is really what you want to do?"

"I'm okay with it. I thought about it during my drive back from Vegas. I'm going to hang on to Mike's shop, let him finish what he's got, and see if he is really planning to leave for Illinois, where Vicki is from."

"Illinois, did he tell you that?"

"He said Vicki could get a waitress job where she worked before, and she'll make good money and the cost of living is cheaper there, and they can kickback. Oh, and he said he'd marry her."

"Chicago must be nice," Elena said.

"Not Chicago. He said it's Springfield, sounds like a town."

"If he really wants to go and you dump the Whittier shop too, you'll be down to one shop, the cow."

"Yeah. I may put another spray booth and oven there and stop all the other bull."

"What about Jose?"

"Jose is a fantastic mechanic. He'll find another place. Sam will make sure of that."

"What about the upholstery shop?"

"Fuck the upholstery shop."

Elena stretched her hands across the small kitchen table, pushing the socks aside, and we held hands. One of the socks rolled off her side of the table. She let go of me, leaned down, and picked it up. I saw her toss it in the air about an inch or two and then catch it like she was gauging the weight. She put the sock back on the table with the others and grinned at me.

"How much you win?"

I smiled, big time. "Let's count it," I said.

***

In the next two days, I deposited ten thousand in my personal checking account at Holmberg's bank that was now being managed by Mr. Graham. I had not yet had word if Holmberg was coming back. I had not written a single company check for months, so Graham had no reason to call me in the mornings threatening to close my accounts. While I was there, I verified the equipment loans were current. They were. The balance in the Eastland account was fifty dollars, so I beefed it up. I deposited a thousand. I didn't stop to see Graham.

I went to Kitty's bank, and with six hundred dollars from my winnings, I paid the past due amount on equipment. Two hundred brought me current on the payment for the ten-thousand-dollar credit line. I deposited a thousand to the Eastland account, an account I had not written a check on since she bounced all the checks.

Kitty had two people at her desk. She saw me look her way. I waved at her and smiled, not revealing how I really felt seeing her.

With eighty thousand in cash on hand, I needed a more secure solution than stashing it in socks. I arranged for the Garfield Safe Company to deliver a sturdy safe with a combination lock to my apartment. After my unsettling encounter with the keeper, I no longer trusted the safe at the office. I couldn't risk having someone come in and freeze everything, including my hard-earned winnings. I had federal and state taxes to contend with, but Eastland needed to provide the funds to cover them. Unlike previous times when I used my Vegas winnings to settle up, this time felt different—I truly believed I had reached the end of my winning streak.

Elena and I went back to work. As far as the world was concerned, I had no winnings in the bank or in cash at home. Everything continued on a cash basis. The landlord threatened to sue me for the breach in the Soto Street lease, but when the for-lease sign went up, the landlord asked me to agree to void the lease I had. The big guy, Earl Scheib, wanted the shop. My agreement was contingent on Earl Scheib or the landlord paying off Kitty for the spray booth, oven, and compressor. They didn't agree right away because Earl Scheib used another type of booth. In the end, I got off. I lost out, but it was one less drain. I gave each employee three weeks' severance pay.

"I'm glad the Soto Street landlord didn't sue you, baby."

"For sure, but I was ready. Fuck it."

With the same attitude, I broke the lease with the car wash shop. I met with the same nice man that I had met before. Like myself, he was in a hurry to make a deal. We did it all in one afternoon. He agreed to let me cancel the lease in return for the spray booth, oven, and compressor that I still owed Kitty's bank for.

We talked on the phone.

"I'm shutting down that shop," I said.

"I can't let you off the loan because you guaranteed it. You owe four thousand and change, plus you owe on Whittier shop."

"For now, the Whittier shop is open. That's a story for another day."

"What do you want to do?" Kitty asked.

"I want to pay you two thousand, and you figure a way to get me off that loan."

Two hours after we hung up, she called back and agreed to accept my offer.

"I took the personal guarantee out from the loan agreement," she said.

"Kitty, thanks."

"One day, we need to talk," she said. "I never thought that by bouncing those checks, I'd lose a friend. It was only business. It was not personal."

"We can still be friends," I said. "I had no deal with you to pay checks if the money wasn't in the bank. I get it."

* * *

I called the landlord at the car wash and told him to prepare the lease cancellation and bill of sale for the equipment I would sign over.

"You are making a killing on this," I told him. "You have a turn-key paint and body shop to lease out now."

Landlord saw it another way. "The remaining months on the lease are much more than the value of the equipment, and you are now off the hook."

"I'm a happy camper," I said. I lied.

* * *

At the main shop, I had changes planned but didn't rush them. The upholstery guys were paying me rent. They saw how I had closed the two shops practically overnight. I was no longer fronting any money to them during slow periods or advancing money for material, and I told them I could not afford to have them be late, not even once, on their weekly rent.

My extra body men were already at Mike's location doing insurance work. The cash cow wasn't doing any insurance work, so I only had two bodymen. Jose was tight with me. He taught me so much about what was under the hood of a car and the undercarriage. I leveled with him about how I needed the room to expand the paint shop, but I wasn't going to push him out. I suggested he speak with Sam about relocating. I promised him a thousand dollars when the time came for him to leave.

Susie and Alexa were sweating their jobs. They saw me let Gil go when I closed Soto Street.

"Alexa and I talked," Susie said, "and we can take a pay cut but don't fire us, jefe."

"I promise you'll be here as long as I'm here. No need for a pay cut."

Elena watched quietly. She made few comments in the presence of employees anymore. I think she was in shock at how fast I was downsizing. Maybe she was wondering about her own future. What future did she have working alongside me? I told her more than once that no matter what, if Elena ever left, it would not be me who sent her away. I couldn't help but think of the Texan who sent her away five thousand dollars richer when they met up. Elena was smart. Maybe the Texan was her safety net. If the Texan was more to her than that, only she knew.

I went to see Molly at the tavern. Molly had a look like no other. She was behind the bar, and I could not help but notice her shirts and blouses opened to display just enough of her ravishing breasts. She was petite, but when she came to the shop those two times, I got a good look at her body. She had a tiny waist, voluptuous breasts, and a way too fine ass.

I asked her for an extra ticket for Elena and begged her to please let me pay for it.

"It's my treat," she said. "Is Elena the pretty brunette that came in here about a phone call?"

"Yeah. She's my girlfriend," I said.

* * *

The day before the boat cruise, I went to the tavern at one in the afternoon when Adrian was working.

"Where have you been?" she said, loud and blustery. She was like that, loud like a foghorn in the bar, but had a beautiful look.

"I've been coming over when Molly is working."

"You could at least show up for lunch once in a while." She picked up a rag and wiped down the counter as she talked to me.

"I've been busy," I said. I didn't mention my son.

I told her about the San Pedro boat cruise. She knew about it, but not that Molly was attending or that she'd given me tickets.

"James told me he's getting a divorce," she said. "He said if he doesn't do it, she will."

"Are you joking?"

"I am not joking."

She stopped plying her rag and looked at me with narrowed eyes. "Are you serious about her or something?"

"I don't know her, but I love her," I told Adrian. We understood each other. She raised her hand, and we high-fived across the counter.

"I want James. I want to have a baby with him. I want him for me. Fuck marriage," Adrian said.

As usual, the music was booming. The place wasn't empty by any means, but it didn't seem like anyone was listening.

"Don't say anything," I said, glancing around.

"Nothing to say," Adrian said. "Nothing's happened yet."

* * *

I told Elena all I knew about the cruise, which wasn't all that much. I knew it included a buffet dinner and dancing under the stars to some popular band.

"The cruise is four hours long. It starts in San Pedro, Long Beach, and goes along the coast, I guess."

"Baby, you go. I don't like boats."

"You lie," I said.

"I'm lying," she said pragmatically. "I like boats, but I'm not going on the boat to watch you drool over Molly."

"Drool? I don't drool." I made a slurping noise out of the side of my mouth that coaxed a smile to her face.

"Go, baby. I'll be at the apartment when you get back."

Chapter 20
Up Close With Molly

It was cold. I had my Alpaca jacket on over the blazer, and I wore jeans, a white shirt, a blue blazer, and white tennis. It was already dark when I boarded. Molly was already there at a corner table filled with ladies, and easy to pick her out as the only one wearing a white sailor hat. The music was playing. A few couples were dancing. The boat had not yet launched.

"You look handsome," Molly said, glancing around. "Where's your friend?"

"She passed."

Molly kissed me, a tap on the lips.

"I'll roam until we get out to sea. I'll catch up with you in a little bit."

"Be sure to," she said. "I want to dance with you up close and personal."

Her smile smacked me like full-body contact from Sonny Liston or Floyd Patterson.

She turned to walk away.

"Molly," I said. It was noisy but not so noisy she didn't hear. She turned around.

"Thanks for inviting me."

She walked back four steps to kiss me again.

"Don't go far," she said. "I never get a chance to tell you when I'm tending bar."

"Tell me what?"

"I've had my eyes on you for a long time."

"That makes two of us," I said.

Her eyes, they were bedroom eyes, mesmerizing.

The boat pulled out to sea. The main cabin was all bright lights over the music, dancing, and buffet. Molly and her friends went through the buffet line. I was avoiding her friends. When she was done eating, I was just beginning to eat at my table by the rail on the upper deck. Molly appeared and took a seat across from me.

"You're not being social," she said.

"Stranger that I am, I don't think it's a good idea to be around your friends." I felt odd eating while she had nothing in front of her. I pushed my meat-filled plate in her direction. "Want something from here?"

"I would, but I ate too much."

She pushed my plate back in front of me.

I began working on a thick slice of roast beef.

"I'm getting a divorce from James," she said. "Everyone who is here knows he's a jerk and a womanizer. I've had it. I've been putting up with his nonsense for most of my married life."

"How long is that?"

"Almost six years."

"James is crazy," I said. "How can he want someone else when he's got you?"

"He's crazy, all right, but he needs to be crazy without me around."

"I hear you." Me going along like this was abusive because I was no different than her husband, at least about being a womanizer.

"I want to dance with you after you eat."

I could see she wanted to dance immediately.

"No time like the present," I said. I abandoned my food, and we went down. "But I'm warning you. I'm a terrible dancer."

The dance floor lights were now dim, and the sea ink-dark with the distant coastal lights twinkling on the water's surface. The ship moved along drowsily, feeling like it was barely moving. They played a slow dance. I had no trouble with slow dancing, and it was good that the floor was filled with couples. I kept my distance, but Molly joked around and pulled me close. The live band extended the song, and we kept dancing. This was happening fast.

Nothing was happening too fast. We were only dancing.

"I'm getting a divorce, too," I said.

"You mentioned that before."

I had mentioned it but provided no details. It wasn't like I lived at home with my wife and daughter and was coming home every night. My home was somewhere else entirely.

"We haven't lived together in a long time. The divorce is something we agreed to a while ago. It is just a paper thing we need to do." A quick flash of my son: We had agreed to delay the divorce until he was born, but we never moved forward to do it. Now that my son was gone, it was going to happen.

"I'm doing it for sure," she said.

At the bar on the upper deck, I got a sparkling water, then another. Molly's way of mixing and dancing reminded me of Sophia. She danced with girlfriends and men who seemed to know her. I never walked over to Molly to ask for a dance, but she found me every once in a while. We danced three dances, one after the other.

When we approached the dock lights, I was on the upper deck. I said good night to her, and her group was below.

"Thanks for inviting me. I had fun."

She kissed me. She spoke to me, not five inches from my lips.

"I want to see you again," she said.

"Seriously?" The question confused her.

"What do you mean?"

"I mean, I'd love to. Are you serious?"

She nodded. "I've been looking at you for a long time. Let's be friends."

"Of course," I said.

"My days are numbered at the tavern. Don't stop coming over while I'm still working there."

"Let me know how to reach you," I said.

"I will."

Another kiss.

* * *

I drove from San Pedro. I stepped into my apartment at one in the morning. I hung the Alpaca jacket in the front closet. The TV was on in the bedroom. I found Elena sitting up in bed naked, watching a rare late movie.

"Baby, you look delicious in that outfit. Come to me just the way you are."

Elena grinned. "This old thing?" she said, moving her hand to indicate her naked self. She seemed jovial, which made me feel good, though I felt guilty that she hadn't gone on the boat.

Elena came out from under the covers. Except for the TV, the bedroom was dark, but there was enough light for me to watch her as she pushed me gently down on the bed. She untied my tennis shoes and dropped them on the floor. I was still fully dressed when she got on me, started kissing me, and gyrated against the eager ridge in my pants. I kissed her back. We hugged and wrestled. Then she slid down my body. I heard my zipper unzipping. She grabbed me there.

I wanted to move freely, but my jeans were constricting.

"Let me take my clothes off, baby."

"No, stay like you are."

She pushed me against the pillows. It was easy to close my eyes and let her take control. She took me in her mouth.

"This is me and you," she said. "Remember."

Not likely that I would forget. When my clothes came off, I gave her the same pleasure she had just given me. It was Sunday. We were awake with the sun, but we'd had very little sleep. We didn't jog, and we didn't get up right away.

"Does she know we live together?"

"She does. She knows you've been my girlfriend for a long time."

For the first time ever, Elena seemed unsure about us. She clung to me. When our eyes met, she wasn't crying. She had the smile, and a stunning beauty all her own. She and Molly were both beautiful, but there was something in Molly that drew me to her.

"Baby, she's married," I reminded Elena.

"That doesn't matter," she said. "When Susie is here with us, I know you dig it, but there isn't the spark in you like when you come back from the tavern."

"Baby, you are imagining it," I said, but Elena was right.

"Do you plan to see her somewhere other than the tavern?"

I remained silent, but she pinched me here, there, and everywhere, Elena's way of making a joke out of the question. It turned physical. Not a fight, something bordering on sexual. I guess it was another level of teasing.

"If I can, yes. I want to see her away from the tavern." I admitted.

"I hate you," she said, rolling away and putting her back to me. All I could see was the back of her head, but I swear, she was pouting.

"Baby, don't hate me."

We were still in bed. I pulled her to me.

"Elena, don't hate me. I need you. You need me."

***

Elena didn't immediately disengage. While I typically followed my own desires, I valued her friendship and appreciated her unwavering support as a sounding board for my ideas and choices. Despite having a lawyer and CPA nearby, it was Elena with whom I sought counsel. She was, above all, my closest and dearest friend.

I continued returning to the tavern in the afternoon when Molly worked. I never stayed long. I didn't want to be a distraction. A waitress worked the tables, but Molly was always busy attending to the bar clientele. It became the highlight of my day to see her, even if we didn't have much time together.

"James stayed out all night with Adrian," Molly said.

"How do you know?"

"When he got home, I confronted him. He got mad and told me he had done it. And he said, 'So what?'"

"Wow, I'm sorry."

"She's not married. It's not her fault. It's his fault." The piped-in music was always playing at the tavern. Molly's voice was so low that I had to lean close to hear.

I had only met James three times. I didn't want to badmouth him. I had no right. I hardly knew him. I had no right badmouthing Adrian. I thought she was a nice woman who said she was falling for a married man who happened to be her boss.

Molly told me that James had been arrested for carrying a concealed weapon, discharging a weapon in a public location, and injuring a person.

"How did that happen?"

"He was downtown at a restaurant with his brother. He said the gun dropped to the floor and went off, and the bullet hit his brother in the leg."

"The brother is okay?"

"He's okay. James is out on bail. I want out of this marriage with him. I plan to leave him. Once I leave him, I'll get a divorce."

I wanted to advise her that she could simply see a lawyer and get the divorce. I thought of how quickly I got a divorce in Mexico but said nothing about it.

*** * ***

Another afternoon, Molly said, "I want to see you."

"That would be nice," I said. It would be more than nice. "Who takes care of your daughter when you work?"

"My mother. I drive her over to my mom's and then pick her up when I leave here."

"What's your daughter's name?"

"Sylvia. She's five. Just started kindergarten."

*** * ***

Elena put on the coffee before she got in the shower. I was dressed and pouring myself a cup of coffee when the phone rang. I answered in the living room.

"It's me, Molly."

"Good morning," I said.

"Back at you," she said with a little laugh. "I just dropped my daughter off at school. We could have breakfast."

"I'm in. Where?"

"How does Montebello sound?"

I dropped Elena off at work and met Molly at Jack in the Box on Garfield in Montebello. It's all part of Los Angeles.

She picked the place, and I was cool with that. It was early in the morning. I saw her cab-yellow car in the parking lot and found her immediately inside, seated at a table for two. The fixed stools were across from each other. She wore a peacoat, and I wore my peacoat, too.

"We're dressed like twins," she said happily. I loved her lips. I loved her teeth. She had a small mole on the side of her nose. I loved it.

We didn't immediately kiss, at least not until I was about to sit.

"You can kiss me." She said.

I leaned down, and our lips met. It was a light kiss, but a kiss just the same.

She told me what she wanted. I went to the counter to order. Molly was right next to me, but I did the talking. We stood in line, waiting. Even the slight pressure of her arm against mine as we waited was exciting to me.

Jack in the Box patrons are in and out fast. It's not designed for leisurely meetings, but we were there for every bit of an hour. Our table was so small that when we leaned forward to talk, our faces were inches apart. We spoke quietly, so only the two of us could hear.

"I liked you the very first time I saw you a long time ago," she said.

"I haven't been going to the tavern that long."

"You didn't notice me in Ensenada? I was with James and another couple."

"Ensenada?"

"You don't remember?"

"I wasn't alone?"

"No, you were with two girls and a guy."

"Molly, you won't believe this."

"I will. Tell me."

"I was there with a girlfriend named Alicia, her roommate, Clara, and her boyfriend. We got married that night after the nightclub." What were the odds of Molly running into me in that place on that day? They had to be astronomical.

"Married?"

"I told you I'm married and getting divorced?"

"That's when you married your wife?"

"Maybe I should get us more coffee."

I should leave it there because it's a hell of a cliffhanger. But the chat didn't end there. It ended with more coffee and more revelations.

I got up. Molly got up with me. We held hands.

When we sat down with our coffee, I told her about Selena, Alicia, and Sophia, my three wives.

"I know you have to be joking. You're how old?"

"Twenty-three," I said.

For the next two mornings, I met her at the same time, same place. It took that long for us to exchange stories.

"My story is nothing in comparison to yours."

"That's a good thing, Molly."

She smiled.

"Is Molly your real name?"

"Everyone knows me as Molly. My name is Amelia. No middle name."

I smiled.

"I like that name. Both are sexy."

"I like sexy," she said with that turn-on smile.

* * *

When I entered the shop, the girls were totally swamped. Thank God for the business. I said good morning to Susie and Alexa.

"You're so chipper," Elena said. "Did you go get a quickie? You didn't get enough this morning from me before we jogged, so you had to go find the married woman to get off again."

That stung. Her one-liners often stung, but Elena never really looked angry. Maybe it was callous of me to laugh, and I wish I hadn't, but she was not fragile. I relied on that when I talked to her, as I spoke freely. She did the same.

"I swear," I said in her ear. "I did not go have a quickie with anyone."

At noon we went up to my office. Instead of lunch, we spent a lust-filled hour of sexual gymnastics that ranged from the sofa to a chair and onto a spectacular floor finale. It's nothing short of a miracle that the office didn't come crashing down into the meat market's refrigeration units.

* * *

That night at the apartment, we were having dinner. Elena seemed distracted. We'd picked up tacos on the way home, and we had just sorted out our plates liberally fringed with dots of salsa, sour cream, and guac surrounding the tacos.

"Is there something wrong?" I asked, wondering if Molly was still on Elena's mind.

"Donald told me that the main shop's days are numbered." She got out the wine glasses, and she poured red wine for both of us.

"He's an alarmist. I think he thinks that the books and records of the business talk to him."

"Baby, you have the money. Pay what you owe, or before you know it, we're going to have that keeper from the state moving in with his bedroll. We're going to have the Internal Revenue Service chaining up the entrances and throwing us all out."

"The money I have is my personal backup. Every win I've had, I came back and used it to put out fires, leaving me with nothing. I'm not doing it. I'm setting aside cash every day to pay the taxes."

"I see you are, but it is not nearly enough. I get this feeling you want the shop shut down."

"I want no such thing," I said. "If they shut me down, at least I have the money to make a final payroll and give out severance pay. More important to me, I have enough to give you a chunk for all you've done for me."

"You sound like you're getting ready to close the door on me."

"I'm only saying that I owe you so damn much that it's embarrassing."

"I get paid every week like everyone else. You owe me nothing. I'm here because I want to be with you. I have a feeling that this married woman will mess everything up."

"Elena, I love you, but from now on, use her name. Stop referring to her as the married woman."

Two days later, on Sunday, Elena packed up her clothes. I fed the fish and was on the living room sofa, taking off my shoes after jogging alone, when Elena walked past me to the door carrying two suitcases. I wanted to help her, but I couldn't help her leave me. I remember a confusion of feelings. Love, grief, exasperation, and relief were only a few of them. Elena was a record. I'd never stayed with the same woman as long as I had with her. Part of me did not believe she was leaving.

"I'm going to my aunt's house. When you want me back, all you need to do is tell me that you are finished with Molly."

So that was it for our apartment. It was back to being my apartment.

I didn't ask Elena if she was quitting. When she left before, she had not quit. Molly hadn't even been around. The last time she had set eyes on Molly was when we painted her car yellow.

Chapter 21
Elena Splits

The next morning Elena was at the shop, but she was not in jeans. She was not dressed to the nines, but she was dressier than the norm and in high heels. Susie whistled when she saw her. Customers paid attention, catching on to the excitement, though they would have no knowledge of why. Alexa whistled too. The department workers were insulated by shop noise from the drama of Elena's entrance.

Elena kissed me.

"Can we go up to the office and talk?"

I nodded and proceeded ahead of her to the office. I held the door open and closed it after she walked through. I expected her to sit down, but she did not.

"I'm going to spring away," she said as soon as we walked in.

"It was lonely without you last night," I said.

"You won't be lonely for long, I'm sure."

"Springing away? Meaning you'll be back?"

"I don't know. I'm headed to Miami. My plane leaves in three hours. I'm leaving my car here. I'll catch a taxi to the airport. Please park the car inside or at your apartment."

"Of course. Is it the Texan?"

"He has a name. I told you before. David."

"Sorry about that."

"Yes, I'm meeting up with David. He has a house there. I need to clear my head."

"Of course. I understand."

I kissed her. She was non-responsive for a few seconds, then she kissed me back.

"Safe travels," I said.

And she was gone. Just like that.

At noon, I drove Elena's Mustang to my apartment and parked it in her spot, next to my parking spot, right below my place. I went up and left the keys in the kitchen.

I kept thinking of Elena's worry that I owed the IRS and State Board of Equalization. We both knew a keeper would eventually come back with his bedroll as before, or the IRS would come and padlock the doors and throw everyone out of the premises. I had the money why fight it?

I opened the safe, took out thirty-five thousand dollars figuring that it had to be enough to pay off what I owed. I took a taxi back to Eastland and called Donald to come over and make the IRS and State Board of Equalization calls for the exact amounts due, then move quickly to get them paid.

I still owed the three check-cashing companies a bundle due in a few months. I owed at least thirteen vendors who provided parts or supplies. As long as I kept buying from them and paying COD, there wasn't much pressure. Every once in a while, I'd get a nasty call from one of them threatening to sue. I could live with that. None of them had bounced checks.

After I paid the taxes, Eastland was no longer on borrowed time. But nothing lasts forever.

I walked across the street to see Adrian at the tavern. Molly was due to clock in in less than an hour. To justify my sitting at the bar, I got a beer. Not many people were there, so Adrian had time to gossip with me. I did not tell her about meeting up with Molly, but Adrian opened up and talked about about spending more time than ever with James. Then she dropped a bomb.

"After he spent the night at my house, Molly came in early," Adrian said. "She asked me to follow her to the back office. We went back there and found Martin, James's assistant doing the books. She chased Martin out of there. She followed Martin to the door and closed it. We were alone. Before I knew what was up, she slapped me, then slapped me again."

I could see Adrian getting upset as she told me this. Her face flushed, and her eyes got squinty, and she deployed the bar rag like a cross between a voodoo doll and a martial arts weapon.

"I slapped the bitch back," she said, slapping the cloth down on the counter. "She punched me so hard, it knocked the air out of my lungs, and I had trouble breathing."

"You're joking," I said.

"I'm not joking. Stay away from James or else," she said. "I pictured foam would come out of her mouth. Work my shift tonight, bitch," she said and walked out.

"Wow. So maybe she cares about him," I said.

"She doesn't care about him. She only wanted to let me know she knew about us."

"Adrian, I'm sorry."

"I told James what she did. He said he's got no control over her."

"So, now what?"

"Nothing. I see James almost every night." Adrian smiled like the cat who ate the canary.

I drank half my beer, put a five on the counter, and gave her a quick kiss when she leaned over towards me before clocking out.

"Hey, you keep leaving me five-dollar bills. We're friends. You don't need to tip me."

I said goodbye and hit the sidewalk.

At a quarter to five, Susie said I had a phone call. It had to be either a creditor, a customer, or Mike. It couldn't be Elena. She was in the air somewhere between here and Miami.

"Hey, you," she said. Before she said a word, I knew it was Molly at the tavern because of the music.

"Hey," I said.

"I miss you. Come over and have a beer."

"I'll be there before you know it," I said.

I couldn't just leave. The hour up to closing time was always busy with customers picking up their cars and others dropping off. But eventually, the traffic stopped, and I was able to walk out. When I got to the tavern, I saw she was very busy. I found a vacant stool and sat down. She'd seen me come in, and I got a smile from her and a beer soon after.

Finally, I got a few words with her.

"I wanted another look at your eyes and hair," she said. "Can't do tomorrow. I'll call you when I can."

"Sure," I said. "No pressure."

She made eyes at me. "But I want to see you."

"I want to see you too," I said.

This picture of her and me bugged me. This angle of my being at her husband's bar flirting and conspiring with his wife about meeting up was uncool. But hey, he was doing the same with Adrian. It was just the mirror reflection of what they were doing. Still, it was not cool of me, and I knew it then and now, decades later.

I returned home alone and retrieved a sheet pan from the cabinet. I unwrapped a massive beef burrito that the chef at the meat market had prepared for me. Back then, microwaves hadn't been invented yet, so the oven was the best way to warm a burrito, achieving that perfect balance of heat and toastiness—unless you opted to pan-fry it. After taking a shower, I put on my sweats. If Elena had been there, she would have devoured half of it, but I left her portion untouched. I couldn't help but wonder if she would call to let me know she made it to Miami. Deep down, I doubted she'd reach out on her first night with the Texan.

I ran a test in my mind. Whenever I thought of Molly, the image of Elena faded away. I wasn't naïve enough to believe that Molly was interested in us as a couple; we'd never discussed it. I knew that married couples could get mad at each other, reconcile, and then get mad again—it's a cycle. As soon as the thoughts of Molly faded, Elena reappeared in my mind. And it made sense; it was only eight in the evening, and I was lying in our bed—I mean, my bed—while she was off with the actual Texan. All I had for company were reruns of My Three Sons, Bewitched, and Peyton Place playing on the television.

My phone rang.

"Elena?" I answered, "It's your nickel."

I heard laughs. "Boss, that's funny. Is that the way you answer the phone at home?"

It was Susie giggling. It was 8:15 pm.

"Hey, long time no see," I said. "I was sitting here thinking of you."

I heard a different voice say, "Were you thinking of me, too?" Alexa.

"I was thinking of both of you," I fibbed.

"Can't kid a kidder," Susie said.

Elena would have said, "You can't con a con."

"I've been staying at Susie's," Alexa said.

Susie said, "We're sitting here, wondering if you're okay all alone there, seeing how Elena is away."

"I'm good. I just had a burrito the size of Mike's shop, and I'm about to chase it with some wine. What you two doing?"

"Waiting to be invited," Alexa said, laughing.

I didn't think Elena had arranged this as she had in the past. But who knows? I didn't need Elena to look after me.

"Come over," I said. "I won't take so much as a sip until you get here."

I got up from the bed and straightened out a few wrinkles on the comforter. I was dressed. I went to the living room. I sat on the sofa and leaned back, eyes closed. I was bothered by something. I think I was heartbroken. Maybe only a crazy man would be heartbroken. Two stunning young ladies were on their way to my apartment. I already knew what they liked, and they knew what I liked.

Maybe they came in a rocket ship. It was fast. They came inside, and when they hugged me, it was like springtime had walked inside.

"We were going to kick back, watch TV, and hit it," Alexa said.

"Yeah, then we thought of you, boss. Are you okay?"

I closed the front door. "I am now," I said with a chuckle. "Make yourself at home."

I led them to the sofa, feeling the warmth of their presence wash over me. The tension that had been weighing on my mind began to lift as we settled in together. The room filled with laughter, and the air buzzed with a lighthearted energy that I desperately needed. I could see the concern in their eyes, but most importantly, I could feel the comfort of companionship. "So, what's on the menu tonight?" I asked as I moved to turn on the Hi-Fi that had a stack of 45s on the changer. Alexa grinned and replied, "We're here for you, G, you tell us." I couldn't help but smile; maybe this evening would offer the distraction I was looking for and a chance to forget my heartache, if only for a little while.

I opened a bottle of wine, the rich, fruity aroma wafting through the air as I poured deep crimson liquid into our glasses.

"G. You and Elena are really into wine, huh?" Alexa said as she watched me pour.

"I dumped Canadian Club. Wine is where it's at. But I'm still learning. Elena is the expert."

Susie said, "Thank you for sharing with us."

"For sure, G. Thank you!" It was Alexa.

Susie had drunk wine with Elena and me before but not Alexa.

I nestled myself between them. We drank from each other's glasses, our lips meeting in soft, lingering kisses, our hands exploring each other's contours. Our clothes were on. We savored the wine slowly, its complex flavors unfolding with each sip. The music in the background was perfect, It wrapped around us like a comforting blanket.

"Are you kiddos hungry?" I asked, breaking the serene silence.

"We're good," said Alexa, her eyes sparkling in the dim light. Susie nodded in agreement, her smile gentle and reassuring.

"There's half a burrito I didn't eat. You two can split it, or I have cheese, salami, and crackers. You know the drill. Want some?" I offered, my voice soft and inviting.

"Are you hungry?" Susie asked her face inches from mine, her breath warm against my skin.

I kissed her. "I'm good," I replied, feeling a sense of contentment settle over me.

I felt Alexa's hand squeeze my upper thigh before she said, "G. Do I get one of those kisses like that?"

A few minutes later we were sittiing on my bed with a whole bunch of pillows against the headboard. The television was on but the volume was off. The music from the Hi-Fi in the living room drifted through the bedroom.

Pages of Passion Book 4: Threads of Destiny

Susie

George Hatcher

Alexa

I get this guilt trip when I skip my jog so I jogged. Susie and Alexa went to work ahead of me to open Eastland. I took my time in the shower and had three cups of coffee instead of one. I missed Elena.

I called Donna's number in Las Vegas. The motel operator answered and connected me. It rang four times, and a sleepy voice answered.

"Hello?"

"I knew I'd wake you. Sorry."

"Is this you, G? Are you in town?"

"No, I'm in Los Angeles. Wasn't sure whether to call in the early evening or at this hour. I wanted to catch you."

"You got me, and I'm happy you called."

"I was thinking about Friday. I was wondering if you might be interested in kicking back with me in my tiny apartment until Sunday."

"Groovy," she said.

"Way to go," I said.

"I don't need to fly," she said. "I have a car."

"I didn't know."

"I use taxis in Vegas because, you know. Vegas."

"I'll be happy to spot you airfare, everything," I said.

"I'd like to drive," she said.

"Go back to sleep. Call me when you wake up."

"I have your card."

"Write down my home number in case I'm not at the office."

* * *

I drove to the shop in a great mood with the radio on way too loud. If Molly happened to call me to meet up, I'd cancel Donna in a heartbeat. There was time before Donna headed over. Molly wasn't going to call.

Once at the shop, I hit the floor and attended to a customer that wanted an idea of what it was going to cost to replace his motor. "If you give me a good price, I'll have it towed over here."

"What did you say your name is?"

"Joe," he extended his hand, we shook.

"Joe, I need to have the car here. Where is the car?"

"Ten minutes away, it's at my house."

"Tell you what, get it towed, and if you don't like the price, I'll pay to have it towed back to your house. Does that work?"

"Hey man, yeah, it works."

"If you have triple A, you get the tow free," I said.

"I ain't got that. Remember your promise."

We shook hands again. "You bet I remember. If you don't like the price, your car will be towed back to your house at my expense."

Now he wanted to fist it, we did, he left.

I loved being my own boss but hated the constant money shortages.

Men are an easy sell when they deal with a good-looking woman like Elena. Susie and Alexa also had the gift, the looks, and the sales talk. A paint job at $35 is what we were after. A $35 paint job and take the dents out was what we really wanted. I heard Susie telling a guy, "I'll do whatever you wish. You want to only do the paint, you will love it, but... You will wish you took the dent out on the door, small as it is, it's going to show."

I attended to another client, so I didn't hear the outcome until later when I saw the bodyman working on the door dent. I said nothing. I smiled to myself. I missed Elena. I would miss her even more at lunch.

I did go by the tavern that afternoon to say hi to Molly, who had just started her shift. I got my daily dose of Molly: the look, the mug of beer, and a little conversation.

"Maybe next week we can hook up at McDonald's in Montebello," she said. "I miss our little breakfast sessions we were having."

I laughed. "I love McDonald's," I lied. "I also miss our breakfast outings. I'll go wherever you want."

After closing up, I drove Susie and Alexa to Margarita's, a popular Mexican restaurant on Brooklyn Avenue, just ten minutes from the shop. We enjoyed a fantastic meal—while the girls each had a beer, I settled for a bottle of Perrier.

"G, do you want to be alone tonight?" Alexa asked. Before I could respond, Susie jumped in, "Jefe doesn't like to be alone."

Earlier, I had thought about reaching out to my neighbors,

Ava and Emma, but I never got around to it. "It would be bitchin' if you came over," I finally said.

I drove them back to the shop so Alexa could grab her car, and Susie decided to join her. They planned to pack an overnight bag and meet me back at the apartment.

That night, we made a huge pot of popcorn and lounged on the bed, watching a movie—though I can't recall which one. Back then, our options were limited. We joked around and had fun, but we didn't have sex. Petting, yes. I was perfectly content just being in their company.

Chapter 22
Donna Visits

Donna arrived at my house on Friday evening, just before seven. I had just gotten home. I met her in front of the building, then got in the passenger seat of her car to show her the underground parking. After she parked in a guest spot, I walked around the car, hugged her, and we kissed like lovers do. I carried her small suitcase, and we entered my apartment from the back.

"This is nice," she said.

"Not like the suites in Vegas," I said.

"I wish I lived in a nice apartment like this."

I showed her around. I thought about telling her about my house that the embalmer was living in and how we gave it up, but in the end, I didn't bring it up. With her living in a hotel room, it would be like boasting. Besides, it was a rental, not my own house.

I showed her the wine rack in the kitchen.

"I want some," she said.

At nine, we were on our way to P.J.'s in West Los Angeles in the first limousine I ever hired. A hundred dollars would cover the cost of the beautiful car, the driver, and the tip for the driver. It was a big luxurious car, but not a stretch. The back seat could have easily seated four. The jump seats were up and out of the way, freeing carpeted floor space between us and the driver's partition.

"What a surprise," Donna said. "Good thing I brought this dress."

The driver dropped us off in the front, packed with cars and people. They didn't accept reservations. I brought a bunch of twenty-dollar bills as my insurance to get a good table and ongoing good service.

I wondered if Kathy and her friends might be at P.J.'s. I had not seen Kathy after our second Hilton visit.

P.J.'s had good wine. I wasn't close to knowing wine, but Donna's taste was right on. She ordered a Chateau Mouton Rothschild, about forty dollars a bottle at P.J.'s. Today, some of the early sixties Rothschild wines run over four thousand a bottle . The wine went slow because we did more dancing than drinking, even though dancing is thirsty work.

"I must warn you, I'm a terrible dancer," I said. It was true and I remember always saying it to someone I'd never danced with before.

"We're going to have fun," Donna said.

Her blue eyes were beautiful. Her blonde cut was all Marilyn and no pixie. We did dance a lot, and it was fun. More importantly, I didn't notice anyone I recognized, and it kept me from thinking of Elena.

By one, we were headed to my apartment. I told the driver we were in no hurry. It wasn't a stretch like are available today, but there was more than enough room for us to make a memory. Yes, we could have waited until we were back at my apartment. We didn't wait, no one saw us and the driver was busy driving. It was a fun night. In a sort of way, just sort of, Donna reminded me of Zoe, the girl I met on the train when I was running away from Juarez. Not the looks. The person.

Sunday noon, I walked Donna to her car and put her suitcase in the trunk. We kissed. It started out a deep, swirly, deeply romantic garage kiss, but we bumped noses in the middle of it, and it ended up with lots of funny little pecks, tit for tat.

"We're real friends now."

"Yes," I said.

"You're an amazing person," she said. "The stories you tell fit a person five times your age."

"That doesn't make me amazing. Just busy."

"Yeah, it does. Busy and amazing."

"Call me and let me know you arrived safe."

"I promise," she said.

* * *

I was tired, but I stripped my bed to the mattress and put it back together with fresh bedding, even the four pillows, not counting the shams. As soon as I was done, the last thing I put on the bed was me.

The phone rang. I thought it was Donna and that her car had conked out.

"Your nickel," I said.

"I miss you," Elena said. "Our Sundays together."

I sat up in bed. It was good to hear her voice. I was full of news and confession and wanted to bare my soul naked. We were always so honest with each other. I wanted to say that she left because of Molly, and Molly was nowhere around me and how I had filled lonely nights with Susie and Alexa and the weekend with the blonde from Vegas, but it was too far a distance between us already, and I said nothing. Maybe when she came home. If.

"Hey, I miss you too."

Chapter 23
Back To Reality

Monday, I called the Whittier Auto Center landlord.

"Just letting you know I'm not going to extend beyond the one year. My attorney is sending you a letter."

"I pass by frequently, and it's always as busy as can be. What's wrong?"

"I get that business from insurance companies who wait four months or more to pay me," I said. "The property is beautiful, but you know that. Knock it down and put up a tall office building."

He laughed. "There you go spending my money."

"Anyway, I thought I owed you a phone call. I have a little less than three months left of the rent I prepaid you."

"Okay, sorry to see you go, my friend."

"I'll be in touch as we get close to the last week."

"George, if you want to stay month to month with the same rent, I can do that. Walk any time you want."

"Thanks. That might help if there's unfinished work in progress at the end of the present lease."

"Let me know."

I had been busy on the floor since we opened. At noon, I missed Elena. I didn't want to face another empty office lunch or go to the meat market alone. I went to the tavern, and there was Adrian opening up the bar. No one was there but us and the kitchen crew somewhere in the back.

"No beer," I said. "A hamburger well done."

"I got it, baby."

"Oh, today I'm baby."

"You are making it happen for James and me."

"I know you don't mention me to James," I said.

"No chance of that."

Elena had said that James was a gangster. He had to be a dummy, either for dropping his gun and shooting his brother in the leg or not coming up with a better story to cover up whatever really happened. I didn't want to go to war with Molly's husband though if I had to, I was entirely capable of it. The mental problem I had, I had no right.

I had Mike meet me at the tavern for lunch. We didn't sit at the bar but found a table so we could talk. I told him I had given notice that I wasn't extending the lease when the first year was over and that we could extend a month or longer if we needed to.

"In that case, I'm going to Springfield with Vicki."

"I can get the lease extended at your house," I said. "You don't need to run away on that account."

"I'll talk with Vicki, but she wants to go back. I'm afraid if I stick around, I'm going to get busted for drunk driving or worse." He grinned, and we shook hands.

"When we get to the two-week mark, I need to have a list of every check you are floating," I said.

"Maybe by then, I'll get them all paid off."

We stood there, grinning and shaking hands. "I'd love that," I confessed.

"Let's sell the receivables to Sam. He should be paid off by now or close to it."

"I'll check," I said. "So far, we've done without Sam."

"Your call, brother."

When we left the tavern, we walked across the street to Eastland, where his car was parked.

"Love you, brother." Big grin, bigger handshake.

"Are we good?"

"Always, brother," he replied.

He got in his car, ignition on. He put his hand out, and we shook. Mike had a thing about handshakes.

Ending businesses is so final. I didn't know what it felt like to go out and buy a plot to be buried in when the time came, but it felt like I was preparing for the end, like for the last hurrah, the big earthquake, the big disaster that you don't know when it's coming, but when it hits, it will be all she wrote. If a miracle happened and Molly and I hooked up, it would be terrible timing. I was coasting. I owed a metric ton of money, but no one was threatening to jail me on anything. I was totally shielded from having done anything illegal. The check cashers that I owed for bounced checks had accepted promissory notes from me and even if I didn't pay them-and I planned to pay them-their legal recourse was to sue me in civil court. The promissory notes erased the criminal threat. I hate to say again that nothing lasts forever, but I knew everything wouldn't always slide off me like I was greased Teflon. I knew I wasn't ten feet tall or bulletproof. When would the reckoning come? And the street smart part of me nagged, was I really immune from prosecution because of the promissory notes I issued and the check holders accepted?

Pages of Passion Book 4: Threads of Destiny

* * *

You might recall reading that I had sent the insurance work we received at Eastland over to Mike at Whittier Auto Center.

Mike called me.

"I have seventy thousand nine hundred in insurance work completed. Did you ask Sam?"

"I'll call him now and call you back."

I called Sam.

"Georgie, are things better or worse?"

"Better, thanks. How much have you gotten back? I have been sending you over the insurance checks as soon as they come in the mail."

"I appreciate that. It looks like I'm down to fifteen thousand and change."

"I know I told you not to buy any more paper, but Mike says he has a chunk, and it would really help."

Sam didn't answer immediately. "Give me till morning. When you said no more, I put the money to work on other things."

"Thanks, Sam. No pressure."

"Son, I didn't say no. I will call you tomorrow."

"You the best," I said. "Oh, wait, Sam. I know beggars can't be choosers, but if you can do it, I can't give up more than ten percent, assuming you take what he's got." I was done handing over the big chunk he took in the past. I'd rather suffer.

Sam laughed. "How much does he have?"

"Seventy thousand nine hundred."

"I'll call you in the morning."

Molly and I were not just king and queen of the fast-food joints. In addition to McDonald's and Jack in the Box, we stole a few minutes at Safeway, the car wash on Atlantic near her home, and once at Pep Boys when she waited for an oil change on her car. We preferred meeting anywhere other than the tavern.

"I'm not going to be working there much longer," she said. She was buying groceries and meat from Jesse and Chris's store, and I was shopping alongside her. After we stowed the bags in her car, she came into the shop. She said hello to Susie and Alexa, and then we went up to my office. The ten minutes we spent up there was the first time our kisses got passionate. My hands roamed a little, and she didn't push me away. Before we walked downstairs, she laughed at the bulge in my jeans.

"Wish we had time," she said.

Molly was one of a kind. I wasn't looking for rapid sex with her. I could wait.

* * *

Back at the shop, Sam passed on buying the receivables. He offered to loan me twenty thousand. I thanked him and passed on the loan.

"Give me a month," he said. "Ask me in a month, and I can probably handle seventy."

"I may take you up on that," I said.

I called Mike and told him no dice on Sam buying the receivables.

"I have a ton of parts to buy and payroll two days from now."

"Can you make it?"

"Yeah, brother, I got it."

"You got Mag answering phones. Put her on dogging the insurance companies, adjusters, and the older receivables. That's what we used to do before Sam."

"She calls, but I'll get on her to do it more often. Thanks, brother."

My shop, the cow, continued to make enough on paint and minor bodywork to carry itself. I had no rent to pay. For that matter, Mike had no rent to pay because I'd paid a year in advance. I had fallen out of love with his shop. I'd chased the landlord to score the lease, but now it was a burden and a time bomb waiting to explode. The taco restaurant never happened. It was sitting there, empty.

One side of my brain told me I was smart, the other side kept reminding me I made many stupid mistakes. I wish I had something to show for all the money I made in Las Vegas.

* * *

I needed to help Mike out. After all, it was my business he was running. He'd done a damn good job of doing that. He never bothered me for money. Mike being self-sustaining, made it easy for me not to worry about the reality of what was going on over there. I'd taught him how to write checks and find a cashier to delay deposits. It wasn't a question of if, it was when it blew up, I'd be the one damaged by the explosion because the account at Kitty's bank for that shop was mine. Mike signed on that account by power of attorney, but the ultimate buck stopped with me.

We had talked about the Kitty situation. Mike had done it with her five times.

"She's thirty-five, brother. That ain't old. And in return, she financed my new car. She spotted me a five-thousand-dollar unsecured personal loan, and when I've been overdrawn on the business account, she calls me to come in to make a deposit and waives the bank fees."

"You been overdrawing my account?"

"Not often, but it happens. Kitty won't bounce a check on me."

"Well, she bounced a whole damn bunch on me," I said.

"Fuck her," Mike said. "Lubricate her first with too many martinis," he said with a fake hiccup.

Chapter 24

The Price of Survival

Kitty and I had reached a fragile truce. I hadn't forgotten the mountain of bounced checks, the financial havoc, the ruined credit, the jail time I'd barely dodged. The memory still burned, a constant, low-grade fever. But I'd *gotten over it*, or at least buried it deep enough to function. I walked into the bank, a knot in my stomach, and felt a sliver of relief when her desk was empty save for her.

"Hello, stranger. Finally, you come to visit," she purred, her eyes, hands, and mouth already a symphony of over-the-top dramatics, all going ninety miles per hour. She gestured to the chair opposite her, a queen on her throne. "Have a seat."

"I know you don't check on me every day," I began, cutting straight to it, "but just so you know, my equipment loan is current, and so is the ten-thousand-dollar credit line."

Her theatrical eyes widened. "I know you're current, George. But when you were pissed off at me, you weren't so current, were you?" The implication hung in the air: *I know your game. I remember your anger. And I hold the cards.*

"That's behind us," I said, forcing a calm I didn't feel.

"You pushed me," she continued, ignoring my attempt to defuse, her voice sharp, "to settle out the car wash equipment for half of what you owed."

A cold truth. "I owe you a favor for that one," I conceded, letting the words taste like ash. "Anything else?"

"Are you here for a loan?" Her tone shifted, becoming more direct, almost predatory. I told myself, *Don't let her upset you. Don't let her win this round.*

"Not exactly."

A smile, painted on, plastic and unreal, stretched across her face. "Oh, you are here for a loan." Her conviction was absolute.

"Sam told me to wait a month before he can buy more receivables," I explained, my voice tight. "Insurance checks come in the mail. I can bring them right in to you, just as I've been doing for several years with Sam."

The fake smile vanished, replaced by something genuinely interested, a glint in her eye I hadn't seen since before the financial apocalypse. "Are you up for lunch?" she asked, suddenly bright. "Bank's buying."

George Hatcher

* * *

I drove us to Judge Black's favorite spot, Steven's Steak House. Kitty downed three martinis before we even got within three feet of a menu. She drank. I didn't. Just as Mike had predicted, Kitty's rigid demeanor softened, then completely dissolved with each glass. Her attitude improved enormously with alcohol, morphing from icy banker to something far more... accessible.

I hadn't been particularly enthusiastic about getting the money on the receivables from Sam, but as the martinis flowed, a desperate resolve solidified within me. Suddenly, I was ready to fuck this woman to get her to "spring" with that loan. I drove us to Alhambra. She specified it, claiming no one knew her there. In the car, she was a whirlwind of talkativeness and brazen, sexy glances. I left her waiting in the car, the scent of gin and cheap perfume filling the confined space, as I walked into a nondescript motel on Main Street to rent a room. The fluorescent lights of the lobby hummed a sordid welcome.

When Kitty emerged from the bathroom, naked and without her glasses, she was a startling vision. Flawless, except for her mouth. My own dirty vocabulary, honed in jails and alleyways, was no match for hers. I am not easy to offend, but her raunchy deluge of words could make a sailor blush. Her crude jokes and explicit demands were something I had to consciously *get used to*, to simply shine on, to compartmentalize.

I worked her over until she begged me to stop, a grueling hour of contorted intimacy in six different positions. It was a performance, a strategic exertion. I didn't let on that I hadn't had an orgasm; it happened sometimes when my focus was solely on pleasing my partner rather than myself. I would get mine, eventually. Christine had taught me well.

So we separated, and I was on the side of the bed, getting dressed, the stale motel air heavy with our scent.

"Did you like it?" she asked, her voice raspy, a hint of challenge. "Was I better than the toddlers you lay?" (That was the G-rated version of what she said.)

"Kitty, you tell me," I replied, my voice flat, refusing to give her the satisfaction of a direct answer, refusing to engage with her cruel barb.

She sprang out of bed, stretching like a cat, a predatory grace in her movements despite the alcohol. "I loved it! Where do you get the energy, the know-how to please like you do?"

I didn't reply. Even if I had, she wouldn't have heard; she went into the bathroom and turned on the shower, the rushing water a sudden, jarring sound. I finished dressing, a strange thought bubbling up: *Is this what Ava and Emma feel like after a date?* I was making it sound like it took a lot of effort to have sex with her. No, no effort at all, physically. But I would have enjoyed it more if she hadn't taken me down, financially, when she'd bounced that mountain of checks.

Sex seemed to have cured her of both her frantic talking and her sexy posturing. When she emerged from the bathroom, dressed and composed, she stared straight ahead, her hands calmly folded in her lap. Only once did I catch her looking at me, a shy, almost innocent smile on her face. She didn't seem drunk or upset, just calm and content. She didn't speak a word all the way back to the bank, and neither did I. I never mentioned the loan.

I dropped her off at the bank's parking lot. The bank would be closing in less than an hour. She blew me a kiss, a surprisingly tender gesture, before walking toward the bank's back entrance, a silent promise hanging between us.

The motel shower had my name on it. I didn't drive back to the shop. I went straight to my apartment, craving the cleansing burn of hot water pelting down on me. A small, self-satisfied smile touched my lips as I lathered my body, acknowledging my performance with Kitty. As much as I missed Elena, I felt a peculiar sense of freedom to do such things without her physically present—jumping Kitty's bones being a prime example. Not that Elena kept track of my every move or controlled me, but without her around, I felt untethered, free to pursue whatever fleeting opportunity presented itself.

It was too late to go back to the shop. I pulled on shorts and a t-shirt and called in. Alexa answered fast, her voice bright, and quickly handed the line over to Susie. I could hear the usual chaotic din of the shop through the phone and pictured the afternoon crowd.

"Can you handle closing, Susie?"

"Yes, boss, you know it."

"I know. Sorry I left you two with the load this afternoon."

"That's our job, boss. Did you have a good afternoon?"

"I did," I said, a faint smile on my face. "Call me when you're ready to close it down."

"Roger, boss."

"We can bring you takeout, anything you want," Alexa chimed in, having apparently listened in. "Want a steak from next door?"

"What do you guys feel like eating?" I asked, a warmth spreading through me despite the earlier encounter.

Susie and Alexa truly looked after me. No, not just sex. I've always written it as it was. We did more fooling around on a bed than actual sex, and when it *was* sex, my satisfaction came from getting them off, and I always did. *Always*. I knew Elena had mentioned that I didn't like to be alone. It didn't matter. Their friendship was genuine. We watched television together while eating takeout, joked around, and I heard their stories, learning to listen more, four nights in a row at my apartment after work. I still remember those nights clearly.

"Are you tired of us?" Susie once asked, her voice edged with a hint of insecurity.

I wasn't tired of them. They were like roommates, and my apartment was all the better for their attention. It was spotless. I even showed them how to make the bed like sailors do, tight and crisp.

"I dig this," Susie had said, marveling at the perfectly made bed.

"Let me get a quarter," Alexa had joked, going for her purse in the living room, ready to bounce it on the taut sheets.

My working neighbors, Ava and Emma, dropped by one evening, and I introduced them to Susie. They'd met once before, a casual encounter on a weekend when Susie was over with Elena and me, but Alexa had never met them. Their visit was short; they had visitors coming over and had to leave. I can't quite recall, but I'm sure I must have thought about Susie, Alexa, Ava, Emma, and me steaming up the bed. But it didn't happen. I would certainly remember if it had.

Not since Patty had I gotten such a bitching massage with coconut oil. The masseuse who had come over one night, leading to my meeting my third wife, Sophia, had been good, but she didn't compare to four hands working on me simultaneously. Today, that's no big deal. Back then, it was a profound luxury. And I reciprocated. I massaged them both, a forgotten skill I hadn't used since Patty.

* * *

The day after my hotel rendezvous with Kitty, she called me at the shop.

"We never discussed the loan to carry receivables," she said, her voice crisp, back to business.

"I figured you were running late. It was a nice lunch."

"Lunch was good," she corrected, a hint of steel in her voice. "I preferred the dessert that came after. So, about the receivables?"

"The way I do it with Sam, I copy the claims we are selling him. Our agreement says when the check comes in on any case we sold him, he gets the money."

"I know about it, but I never examined the details. How much does he charge?"

"I told him that from now on, it's ten percent. In the past, it's been more."

She laughed, a genuine, uninhibited sound this time. "Maybe that's why he passed."

"Could be," I said, but didn't agree. "You know him better, so you should know he's a straight shooter. He didn't pass. He said a month."

"I agree. He's not only a straight shooter, he has more money than any other depositor at this branch." She laughed again, a light, almost girlish sound. I didn't laugh, but I faked a chuckle.

"Bring me over thirty thousand worth," she said, her voice

firm, back to the banker. "And I'll see how I can incorporate it into a fast loan."

"Mike's shop is doing the work, and he has the paperwork. Can I have him bring it over to you and maybe take you to lunch?" I cleared my throat pointedly, making sure she knew I understood the unspoken implications.

"Yes, have him call me. I'll do this. Thirty to start."

"Kitty, seriously, that is a very cool gesture on your part."

"It's business," she corrected, a note of warning. "I know the deal is clean, or Sam would have been screaming by now, and I would have heard about it."

"You see, Kitty, there you have it."

"When are we going to lunch again?" she asked, a softer edge returning.

"I'm ready anytime," I lied, the words tasting like victory.

I called Mike and told him.

"I told you," he said, a triumphant note in his voice. "Do you need part of the thirty?"

"Damn straight," I said. "Put half in the bank account. Have her deposit the other half to the Eastland account. Get her to do it right away."

"Okay. If you call and I'm not here, I'm out going beyond the call of duty."

"Bull," I said, remembering the quickie Elena and Mike had. "You love to fuck."

Chapter 25
New Circles, Old Tricks

After shuttering two shops and narrowly dodging the Sheriff's Department over a couple of bounced checks, you'd think I'd have developed an allergy to important people. But I didn't seek them out; they seemed to find me. And yes, when I was around them, I was impressed. In my shoes, you would have been too. Could I have done without the reflected glory? Sure. But it was a potent distraction from the abyss I was skirting every single day.

Judge Black phoned me regularly, our conversations a strange blend of mentorship and confession.

"How are you holding out, Georgie?" he'd ask, his voice a low rumble.

"Judge, if you ran a credit check on me, you'd never want to talk to me again," I'd reply, the honesty a relief.

"Nonsense. You went too fast, that's all. You will bounce back. Stay positive and don't be as hard on yourself as I hear in your voice." That was the meanest, most feared Judge in East Los Angeles, offering me fatherly advice. The irony wasn't lost on me.

I couldn't keep declining his invitations to Rotary or Lions Club meetings. I'd put on a suit, a costume of legitimacy, and attend as his guest. My stomach would churn with the fear of running into a creditor who had me on a cash-only basis, but thankfully, that collision of worlds never happened. I'd pass out cards for the "cash cow" shop, collecting as many as I gave out, playing the part of the successful young entrepreneur. The judge, deeply connected, would hit me up for political contributions, even knowing I was struggling.

"I know you have a hundred dollars," he'd say, a command disguised as a statement.

"I wish I could give you more," I'd reply, peeling the bill from a dwindling roll. A hundred dollars back then felt like eight hundred today.

Through Judge Black, I met Luca, a bail bondsman with a booming laugh and an ever-present styrofoam cup of coffee from Winchell's. I painted at least four cars for his family, never charging him a dime. Most of the time he'd drop by needing a new tire or a minor fix, and I always came through.

"I got your back," he'd say. "Whatever you need, just holler."

"Yeah, right," I'd joke, a dark humor coloring my tone. "You're just waiting for me to end up in jail so you can bail me out."

"Kid, you got it wrong," he'd laugh. He was a good friend.

But his friendship also came with a price. One visit, he was raising money for Pablo, the mayor of Tijuana, who was running for Governor of Baja California. Luca pressed harder than the judge.

"Two hundred works," he said.

"I'll give you cash."

"No cash. Has to be a check."

My blood ran cold. The last thing I needed was a bounced check to a politician. I wasn't floating checks at that precise moment, but the fear was constant. Still, saying no to these men was a skill I hadn't yet acquired. I dressed up, I showed up, I wrote the check. That's how I met Pablo. I wanted to tell him about the living hell of his city's jail, but that was a ghost from a past administration. Pablo, I would later learn, was a different kind of animal entirely.

One connection led to another. Judge Gonzales from the downtown courthouse, after a few freebies, referred me to two other judges, and I lost track of how many clerks and marshals followed. The free work went to the judges; discounts went to the staff. As a young man, down and out but surrounded by power, I'll admit it: I liked the attention. It was a dangerous, intoxicating illusion of success.

* * *

While I was rubbing shoulders with the law, Mike was drowning. He called me, his voice strained. "This insurance work is a killer," he said. "Two of my check-cashing places have cut me off. I'm down to one, and I need another fifteen thousand to make it."

The old, familiar poison seeped back into my veins. "Eastland gobbled up the fifteen," I told him, the lie coming easily. The truth was, my own shops were barely breathing. I laid out the desperate, familiar scheme. "Write out thirty checks for five hundred. Give them to your people, your secretary included, and have them cash them like paychecks. Markets, liquor stores, anywhere. Let them keep a little for their trouble."

"And how do I cover the thirty checks?" Mike asked, a humorless laugh echoing down the line.

"Three days later, you do it again. Write another batch, get the cash, and deposit it to cover the first wave." The mechanics of the check kite felt as natural to me as breathing.

"I know how it goes, brother."

"Are you still planning to move to Springfield?"

"Brother, if I didn't love you so much, I'd already be there.

I'm waiting until the lease is up and the cars are finished."

"You're a good friend," I said, the irony thick enough to choke on. "Loyal and oozing with integrity."

"Tell me something I don't know, brother." I could picture his grin, and in that moment, I missed the simple honesty of a handshake.

It was a survival tactic, born of desperation. There was never any intent to let the checks bounce, only to exploit the five-day float—the gap between when a check was cashed at a market and when it finally hit the bank. It was a high-wire act, a frantic dance to stay one step ahead of the inevitable crash. The modern world of payday loans is a sanitized version of this grimy hustle, but the principle is the same: borrowing from a future you're not sure you'll have.

Chapter 26
Molly

I got a call at the shop announced on the intercom- Susie's voice. I picked up the line, heard the background bar noise, and knew it was Molly.

"Can you come to the tavern? I'm here."

"Sure," I said, looking at the clock. It was closer to noon than four." You're way early."

"You don't need to rush," she said.

It was dark inside the tavern. My eyes needed a few moments to adjust. As someone followed me in, the front door opened, sunlight poured inside, and I caught Adrian's expression. I heard Molly's voice right beside me.

"I'm over here." She was at a table near the front door. Adrian was at the bar.

Now, why would Adrian and Molly be here at the same time and that close to each other? I didn't have time to think about it.

"Sit here," Molly said. "I'll be right back in a minute. I need to see Martin."

I knew Martin was James's assistant. I'd never met him but had seen him. I didn't sit, just stood there waiting for Molly's return. My eyes were getting accustomed. I was able to make out Adrian as she winked at me.

"Why are you working when she's working?" I said in a low voice.

"Changes," she said and winked again.

Molly came out of the office.

"Sit next to me," she said, patting the seat.

I slid into the booth, and our legs touched. I jerked from the sensation of contact, but there was no room. I was at the seat's edge, and Molly didn't seem to want to move over.

Okay. Two could play that game. I slid closer, put my arm next to hers, and let our thighs touch. She smiled right into my eyes. All I needed was for her husband, James, to walk in the door. I wasn't afraid, but my position was to my disadvantage. I was wrong, doing what I was doing at his tavern. At least the sunlight was in my favor.

Afraid to ask, I sat still and experienced her warm thigh against mine. At last, she spoke, and it was a bombshell.

"James just got sentenced to six months in jail," she said. "Before he's settled in, he'll be served with divorce papers. It's all over between us."

I took a deep breath and slowly let it out.

"Jail on the charge of shooting his brother?"

"Yes, possession of a gun and who knows what else."

"Got it," I said.

Molly continued. "He called me twice while he was being booked at the county jail. I told him I wasn't coming to the tavern to work as a barmaid anymore. I told him I have seen a lawyer, and he would be served." She sipped her beer, raising her glass, and clicked my mug, then said, "He didn't put up a fight. Told me to come see Martin, which I just did. He said he would give me a hundred dollars a week and pay the rent and utilities on our rented house. I told him I'd take the hundred a week, but our daughter Sylvia and I are moving out."

"Wow," I said as I always do when I'm at a loss for what to say.

"Sorry for being so long-winded."

In spite of the apology, she wasn't long-winded, but she was very, very pretty. The more I was around her, the more intoxicated I got, and not from the beer.

"Are you okay about this? I mean, about the divorce. I'm thinking of your daughter Sylvia."

"He loves his daughter, and he can see her. I'm not taking Sylvia away from him. He's never home very much, anyway, not when she's awake. It will be like there's been no change."

I must have been gaping at her, but I couldn't take my eyes from her face or make my tongue move. I was transfixed by possibilities. A wild hope exploded to life inside me. I wasn't sure what that hope was, but my thigh burned where it touched hers.

We would have been better off in my office at the shop than sitting in James's Tavern with his side-kick Adrian spying on us from a few feet away at the bar. I tried to kick the self-consciousness. I didn't want beer. I craved a good glass of wine.

"Is Elena back?" Molly asked.

"No. She's still out of town."

"Are you committed to her?" Molly asked

"We are not exclusive to each other. She's still in Miami, Florida, with a longtime admirer who I understand is very rich."

"I'm glad," Molly said. "I don't want to break up anything."

She touched my hand that was holding the mug of beer.

"Let's see. You've had three wives, one you are waiting to divorce, plus Elena, plus whatever girlfriends you've had and not mentioned. Who got all your love?"

"I used to think, Selena, my first wife. I'm not sure anymore. I don't know how to measure love. I wonder if anyone does."

"Good point," Molly said. "You're so smart."

"If I was so smart, I'd be loaded with money."

"You look smart to me. Not that I know about business. Business is not what I'm good at. My only job was at Sears in the mailroom, and that wasn't for long. My other job, tending bar, was a job with no pay. But you know business. You have that big corner a few feet away and another shop on Whittier. What are you aiming for?"

"I was forced to close two shops to keep them from burying my main shop, which is the one next door. I'm aiming for success."

"That just proves you're smart," she said, taking a sip of beer.

"Do you think I'll be able to see you more now that you are sort of free?" I asked her that.

"Believe it. That is if that's what you want."

I wanted to hug and kiss her right here in front of everyone, not the smartest impulse.

"I want," I said.

"There's your answer."

We clicked mugs, huge smiles on our faces.

"Did I ever tell you that you have the most beautiful hazel eyes and that your curly hair is a total turn-on?"

"You just did," I said. "Did I ever tell you that you're more desirable than any woman I've ever known? You're beautiful, Molly."

"You think I'm beautiful?"

"I don't just think so. You are beautiful. It's a fact," I said.

Molly's brown eyes stared into mine. I wasn't transfixed or hypnotized; I just wanted to fall into them. She clasped my hand under the table. The next thing, we were kissing very softly. It just sort of happened, like the kiss took us over. I mean, one minute I was trying hard to remember this was James's tavern, and the next, Molly and I had been kissing for who knows how long. It was like we were alone, hidden in a cloud of bar noise, the clanks of glasses, background voices, piped-in music. I heard a glass break, cutting through our cloud, shattering our isolation into a thousand, thousand pieces.

Molly's lips moved on mine

"I think Adrian has noticed."

I glanced at Adrian, who was sweeping the spiky half of a thin-edged pilsner glass from the counter.

We nuzzled each other, cheek to cheek. Witnesses weren't bugging me any longer.

"You know, George, today's my birthday," Molly said.

"You're my birthday present. Maybe we should go out and celebrate."

I put my arm around her and really kissed her. She responded, wrapping her arms around me. Another glass broke. Adrian again. We drew apart.

"That's our signal to get out of here," I said.

We moved toward the front door, arm in arm. As we passed the bar, Molly waved. "Bye, Adrian," she said. "Check the visiting hours at the jail. He'll be happy to see you."

Adrian's face was frozen as in shock, and she was speechless. I winked at her. She should be happy that James would be free soon. There was no denying how alluring Adrian was, something I would never say to Molly. Adrian didn't hold James at gunpoint to cheat. It was James's fault. I would have to let Molly know I wasn't a saint, maybe no better than James.

We stopped beside Molly's car in the parking lot and arranged to meet at my apartment in an hour. I told her how to get there and gave her the address. Molly wasn't going straight there. She wanted to go home to change clothes. So, did I.

As I shaved and showered, I realized that what I wanted was to marry Molly. I had confidence that someday I would really make it big. It wasn't going to be easy. I wanted Molly to have a great big house and everything that she deserved. I would bedeck her in diamonds and furs, be good to her always, take her everywhere with me, and let her know that I loved her. Making the money to do all this was something I knew I could do. I'd find a way. The hard thing, and I knew it, was being faithful to her. Could I do that?

Molly would be different. She would be a real wife. Her love would give me comfort. I was tired of using people, especially women. I needed a full partner to share all of my life with. Elena had been a good partner, but in my mind's eye, instead of seeing her with me, I saw her with Mike, and with the Texan. Elena needed the spring-away clause in our relationship.

I am making it sound like it was Elena who messed it all up. That's just not true. I did my own springing away, often without leaving the zip code. I saw myself attached to Ava and Emma. I saw myself attached to Susie and Alexa, and the married lady Kathy with a K. I sprang to Donna from Vegas. I often thought about Zoe, the girl on the train from El Paso.

Molly was eighteen months older and all grown up. I could not imagine that anything could go wrong between us if she let me have her for keeps.

We had dinner in Hollywood at Don the Beachcomber. While waiting for our table, we sat in the corner of the bar. Over drinks, Molly wrote on the wide-brimmed shade covering the candle: "Molly and George, forever." In one afternoon, we had gone from never talking about a relationship between us to forever.

"That's going to be engraved on our wedding bands. Forever," I said.

She looked at our hands joined on the tabletop, to my eyes.

"Are you proposing?"

"Yes," I said.

She leaned her head down so that her golden hair spread over the table and sparkled in the candlelight.

"I love you," she whispered. "I'll marry you."

Selena, Alicia, and Sophia had not said yes that quickly. Molly and I were in love at first sight.

That night, when I carried her to my bed, I had already married her in my heart. I had never felt such peace with anyone and so much at peace with myself. She may not have been the first girl I truly believed I loved, but she was the first woman, and she would be the last. As I write this, we've been married fifty-five years. You are reading Part One of a story that will have three parts. Marrying Molly was really the beginning of my adult life.

I wasn't sure if she would get pissed for me speaking frankly, but in the morning, before Molly left my apartment, I said, "Don't take this the wrong way. If this thing that happened between us was just a way to get even with James, you got even last night. If you have second thoughts, I will understand."

"James and I were finished long before you and I came together. Don't feel any guilt or think you broke us apart."

"He will think so," I said.

"Do you care if he does?"

"I don't care," I said. "I hardly know him."

She kissed me.

"I'm going to try very hard to change," I said.

"What do you mean?"

"Just take a look. I'm still married. I was living with Elena and have a number of other relationships going on at the same time. If I move outside and look in, I'd say I am worse than your husband James."

"You said this before. I get it. I'll take my chances," she said.

"I'm going to try hard," I said.

She kissed me before she said, "You better."

Next time, maybe I would ask her if she wanted to jog with me, now that I knew there would be a next time. As I showered, I wished that my feeling of doom would go away. Bad things were on the horizon. It was a bad time for Molly to enter my life.

Molly wasted no time moving out of the house she had shared with James. I saw her every day and many nights, but I did not help her move or offer her any help. She had to do it on her own. Even my fish took to her, taking the food from her hand and then letting her pet them.

Elena called me at the shop. I took the call upstairs in my office. No doubt Susie or Alexa had told her I wasn't taking them home any longer, that Molly was dropping into the shop daily. They were probably telling her every time we had lunch in my office or next door at the meat market.

"I knew she was bad news," Elena said.

"Don't be like that. You're totally free from me in Miami right now. I'm here in the same boat. The difference is that Molly and I are serious. I believe we are in it for the long haul."

Elena laughed. "You mean you plan to marry her? Another marriage?" In her voice, I could hear the count of my marriages, even though she had not said it aloud.

I felt my face flush.

"Elena, you should wish me well, not poke fun at my track record."

Long silence.

"You're right, G. I apologize, especially for laughing. I respect and love you too much to be so mean. Shame on me."

"Thanks for that, Elena. I treasure our friendship and always will," I said emotionally. It felt like we were really saying goodbye.

Later that day, I told Molly I had sprung it on Elena.

"Don't tell me what she said," Molly said. "Unless you want to."

I didn't tell her.

My relationship with Molly continued to grow. The bonding felt so natural. There was a sense of rightness and wholeness about it all. When I met Molly's little daughter, Sylvia, it took her a couple of hours to get over her shyness, but we became mutual admirers when she did. One night, I took Molly and Sylvia to a pier-side amusement park in Santa Monica. The three of us rode the rides and yelled up a storm from the Ferris wheel with the ocean below us.

"I'm going to buy a house on the sand one day," I told Molly and Sylvia.

"No pressure," Molly said. Sylvia approved the idea of having a beach house.

Molly invited me to a birthday party, where she introduced me to her many brothers and sisters, their wives, and husbands. I shook hands with countless nieces and nephews. Her family was at least five times bigger than Sophia's. Many years after this, Molly's entire family had a reunion at Whittier Park, and I believe it was like closing the park just for the big event. It was packed with family.

It has become an annual custom for me to cook for more than two hundred family members on Christmas Day.

"I'm happy you are marrying my daughter," my future mother-in-law said. "She's had a very sad life with James."

Molly and Sylvia were living with Grandma near City Terrace in East Los Angeles, ten minutes from my apartment.

Chapter 27
Hard Times

I don't know what started the avalanche. Maybe after I closed the car wash shop and the shop next to Sears, my former employees must have filed for unemployment.

Before closing the shops, I took everyone off payroll and started paying them as outside service contractors. This was not the first time. Employees liked it because I took no deductions, and they took home more money. For me, it cut the employer contributions I had to make. Well, this was wrong of me to do. I knew it, how could I not know it, my CPA was on me all the time about it.

These days, Uber and Lyft are being pressed to stop paying drivers as independent contractors. The government considers drivers to be employees. Deductions should be taken from their paychecks, and Uber and Lyft must pay the employer contributions. In November 2020, Uber and Lyft had a major victory by winning a ballot measure that exempts them from a California labor law.

I was not them, nor am I now, Uber and Lyft with deep pockets. I could not fight an assessment levied upon Eastland Auto Center for the months of work all employees had not been paid through the payroll, plus penalties and interest.

Donald said, "I told you so."

I had little warning that the Internal Revenue Service and the State of California were going to make a move on Eastland. I read every notice I received in the mail. I had twenty thousand dollars at home from the last Vegas winnings, which I would have used to cover the taxes and penalties I owed for having taken my employees off the payroll. The problem was that twenty thousand dollars was not enough to cover it.

Figuring doomsday was soon, I stopped paying the State Board of Equalization the sales tax I collected on each job we did. If the job was all labor, there was no sales tax, but ninety percent or more of my jobs had sales tax for something.

One morning, I handed Susie, Alexa, Luis, and Jose each an envelope with a thousand dollars as severance pay and two hundred to cover about a week of payroll in the event a tax agency shut me down. I couldn't afford to severance all my employees like I did when I closed the other shops. I was out of money.

"Don't spend the money," I said to all of them. "I don't know when this is going to happen, but it will happen, and you will need the money when it does."

At a random time of day, when we were both on the shop floor, and no one else was in earshot, Susie approached me. "Boss," she said, "I would love to do something for you."

"I would love you to do something for me, but it's not a good idea."

"It's Molly, huh?"

"In a way."

"We can slip upstairs or anywhere you like," she said.

I kissed her right there, standing on the shop floor.

"I love you, Susie."

"I love you more, G."

Later, Alexa asked, "Boss, no quickies either?"

I lightly pinched her cheek. "I never say never," I said.

I did try.

Luca called me about a donation.

"I'll give you a hundred for the cause, but soon I will be shut down."

George Hatcher

"Did you tell the judge?"

"There's nothing he can do. I need to pay it or else, and frankly, I don't want to pay it. If I get straight, something will happen in a couple of months, and I'll be in the hole again." I thought of my windfall winnings in Vegas.

Luca told the judge, and the judge called me. I told him the same thing.

"Until it happens, Judge, is there anything you need done while my team and I are still here?"

"You said you are winding down. Whittier Boulevard too?"

"Very soon, the year will be up. I paid a year's rent in advance. I don't plan to go beyond that. The landlord said I could pay him month-to-month if I needed to be there. If they shut Eastland down, I'll go over to Whittier. Mike is leaving soon to go back East."

"What's next, Georgie?"

"Maybe another shop," I said with a laugh.

Judge Black did one of his growls, a laugh that reminded me of Matt, except I don't remember seeing Matt laugh.

"Don't give up," he said. "You have your entire life ahead of you. I love you like my son."

How can I forget Judge Black telling me he loved me?

* * *

The Internal Revenue Service shut down Eastland Auto Center. They don't use keepers who move in. The keeper from the State had warned me about the IRS, and he was right. They just throw everyone out and chain it up. I was expecting it, so how can I say it was a surprise? But it was a surprise because it was real and tangible. Even my buddies Chris and Jesse knew it was coming because I told them.

"I'm sorry. I wish I had the money to help you open it up again," Molly said.

I hugged her. "I told you this was coming. I could have hustled the money, but I'm burned out on playing rescue."

I drove to Whittier Auto Center and relieved Mike of the shop. He seemed very pleased to turn it over to me. He had twenty thousand floating, but all the small checks he had given employees were history and had been paid. He was doing business again with two check cashing places, juggling a total of twenty thousand. It's not hard to juggle that amount with a place that cashes checks for a living. I gave Mike a check for five thousand and told him to cash it. I'd add it to the float. It was the least I could do.

"Brother, I have been saving. I'm cool. I don't need this."

"Yeah, you do."

Mike and his fiancée rented a U-Haul truck, packed all the furniture I'd bought for them when I leased the house and split for Springfield. With the rented truck, Mike towed Vicki's car. Vicki followed in the bigger car.

I would see Mike again, but not in Los Angeles.

Molly knew the whole story about Mike and me and where we met. She was with me when I said goodbye.

"This is a big shop," Molly said of Whittier Auto Center.

"It is, but people don't stop here to paint their cars like at Eastland. If it did, I'd keep it and make a good living on it."

"But you have a lot of cars being worked on."

"They're insurance jobs," I said, then explained the money issue with insurance jobs.

"Doesn't sound good that you have to wait for your money."

"It's not good," I said.

The thirty thousand Kitty loaned on the receivables was almost paid off. The insurance work Mike had not been paid for amounted to fifty-one thousand. If Sam bought those, I'd have some serious money to pay the float with check cashers and leave at least half.

My closest friends encouraged me despite Eastland's failure. Their reassurances were important to me. Although I still felt very insecure, my friends stood by and encouraged me.

"You'll make it in something else," Judge Black said. "Maybe this shop on Whittier will be your saving grace. It's gorgeous. What a layout."

"It doesn't have the draw."

"Win some, lose some," Luca Valle, my friend, the bail bondsman, said, shrugging and grinning at me. "I have donuts in the car; come on, you can have your pick."

As we walked together to his car, laughter filled the air. Memories of Elena and our delightful outings to Winchell's Donuts flooded my mind, reminding me of our shared love for those sweet treats.

You already know I hated being alone, and luckily, most of the time, I wasn't. I was glad Molly was with me every day. I was able to put off my negative thoughts until after Molly went home late at night. Eastland's demise led me to make a running list of the wrong moves I made that led to the death of my shop. In time, I accepted that I had made mistakes and was determined to learn from them.

I started to look for a new location. Whittier was temporary. Nothing new was coming in. Mike had already stopped taking insurance work before I took over. I was there just to finish the last of the insurance work and shut it down.

When Pablo Guzman was elected governor of Baja California, he left his office as mayor of Tijuana. The Mexican American Business Group in Los Angeles sponsored a congratulatory ball at the Century Plaza Hotel in Los Angeles. I bought two tickets. At the tux place, I found out you could buy as well as rent, so that is what I did. I bought everything that I needed, including patent leather shoes. Of course, my date was Molly. She wore a fancy long dress. I wore my tuxedo.

We didn't plan to sit with Judge Black, but he arranged it. Luca and his wife Melissa, three other couples, including a Captain from the Sheriff's Department and his wife, were at our table. I introduced Molly as my fiancée.

The first of Pablo's dinners I had attended had been to raise money for his campaign. I spent a lot of time with him the first time, speaking to him in Spanish. At the time, I was with Elena. This was my second time attending a dinner for Pablo, and it was in celebration of his win. After his speech, the governor made the rounds of the guests with his wife and team. Eventually, he headed to our table, where he saw Luca, Judge Black, and me. He remembered me, and he may have remembered Elena if she'd been there. Who wouldn't?

I introduced him to Molly.

"Soon as we get divorced, we're getting married."

"Come to Mexico and get it done right away," he said, chuckling. He didn't know I had already done it that way before.

"There's a beautiful place on the beach, Guaymas," he said. "A romantic place. If I was going to marry my Lupe again, that's where I would take her."

"I'll remember that. Thank you, Governor."

He shook my hand and kissed Molly on both cheeks. I kissed his wife the same way.

We stuck around for the dancing until everyone at our table started to leave. Judge Black hugged me like I was his son. It felt good. His wife, June, was a sweetheart. I got a hug from her. Molly got hugs all around when we said good night.

Afterward, we were in the car on our way to drop her off at her mom's, where Sylvia was. Traffic was heavy. We waited at a light, and when it finally changed, I could only go a few car lengths. I was still pretty jazzed from the experience.

"The IRS padlocked my shop doors. They are dismembering Eastland and auctioning off the bits and pieces next week. And tonight, we were at a table with some very important people and exchanged conversation, hugs, and kisses with the governor of Baja and his wife. I find that unbelievable."

Molly messed with my hair. I didn't tell her Elena used to do that too.

"Everyone at the table liked you, even the two couples you hadn't met before," Molly said.

"I was sitting with a captain from the Sheriff's Department. If only he knew that once upon a time, I spent months in the old county jail waiting for trial on a grand theft charge that sent me to the Youth Authority."

"That sounds better than when you call it prison."

"I love you," I said.

"Stop the car, and let's exchange our own vows right here and now."

"If I wasn't on the freeway, I would." I laughed.

"Chicken," she said.

"You really are game," I said with a chuckle.

"Try me," she said.

* * *

There was good news. Graham was gone from my world. My favorite banker, Holmberg, returned to the branch. I went to see him after the IRS held the auction.

"Why didn't you put your lien in for the spray booth, oven, and compressor?"

"The loan was too small," Mr. Holmberg said. "I wanted as much as possible to go to your tax debt."

"You're too good," I said.

"I'm sorry about all that went on while I was away," he said.

"It is your life that has been torn," I said, trying hard not to stir up the tragedy. "I wish there was something I could do for you, but I'm glad you're back."

* * *

I left the bank and went to see my friends at the meat market. At the IRS auction, Jesse and Chris had bought the contents of my shop as a package for fifteen thousand dollars[1].

"You scored," I said.

"It's a lot of money to us," Jesse said

It was after hours, and the customers were gone. They didn't look like men about to open a paint shop. They were in their butcher aprons. Chris was in the process of moving items from the front into one of the walk-ins. He came back in and wiped down the display area, talking as he worked. Jesse came out of the back with a package wrapped in white paper and handed it to me-a steak. I thanked him.

"You realize that what you bought are the contents," I said. "I still have the lease. And it is current, so there is no beef with the landlady."

Chris said, "We know that. Look, give us the fifteen thousand, and jump back in."

"Yeah, do that," Jesse said. "We miss you."

---

1. $15,000.00 in the sixties is equal to $124,744.66 in 2020.

"You guys," I said. I felt a little choked up that they had done that for me. The problem was, I wasn't sure the Eastland shop was where I needed to be.

* * *

In the morning, I went back to my Whittier Shop and walked around the office. In the background, the hammering, grinding, and the noise was a constant. I was so accustomed to the shop noise that it was invisible. I knew it was there, but I didn't hear it. I was considering the brothers' offer. I had more than enough to pay them the fifteen thousand they paid the IRS for the shop. I had receivables that were not sold to Sam or borrowed against Kitty and five jobs being worked on at Whittier.

What should I do? Should I go back to the cow? I was on the horns of a dilemma.

I mentioned the problem to Molly.

"You told me you could have hustled the money to stop the IRS from shutting you down, but you didn't really want to do it."

"You're right. If I had wanted to save Eastland, I could have. What happens is that I bail it out, and three or four months later, it needs another bail. That's why I let it happen."

"Your friends are giving you a generous offer, and you are tempted. You want in. You plan to find and open another shop to paint cars. Why look for another place when you can get this one back?'

"If I get another shop, it will be across town, near Hollywood in West Los Angeles."

"Can you paint more cars over there?"

"That or charge more."

Molly put her arms around my waist and looked up at me. I wasn't that much taller than she was.

"Honey, you're the doctor. It's your call. Sylvia and I are low overhead. Don't worry about us."

"I love you," I said, hugging her.

"I can go back to Sears," she said. "I'm sure they would hire me back."

"No way."

The Whittier Shop was closed. I had no plans to take on any new work. I only needed to finish the remaining insurance work and get out. I spent a day there without opening the shop, as my bodyman in charge had keys.

Still uncommitted, I decided to sleep on it. That meant I spent a sleepless night, tossing and turning, and when I did get to sleep, my dreams were anxious rather than restful. Early the next day, I went straight from my apartment to see Jesse and Chris at the meat market. It was early enough that they hadn't opened up for customers yet, but the fragrance of coffee was already in the air.

I told them, "You won't have a problem renting the body shop. It's turnkey. What you need is my lease. That protects your business and the body shop."

Chris reminded me right away that they had a sublease from me. "We're protected," he said.

"Technically, I could open the place up on my own," I said. "I have the lease. The equipment is yours now, but the lease is mine."

Jesse and Chris looked at each other. I knew I had them. "Here's what I'll do," I said. "I'll go see Mrs. Goldberg. I'll tell her that I couldn't manage it, that I want to sell you the lease, and I need to address the option for five years."

"Get that for us for the meat market and body shop," Jesse said, "and we'll give you five thousand."

I laughed, suppressing an urge to yawn. "Which one of you made the coffee this morning?" I asked.

Chris poured me a cup, which brought me back to life.

"I'll get you ten years, and the rent will be fabulous. With any luck, you might get enough rent from the body shop to cover your rent."

"Yeah, like you did to us."

"You have a lease now, no matter what."

"How much?" Jesse asked.

"Twenty thousand," I said.

"What if you can't deliver?" Jesse asked.

"If that happens, we'll explore another option between us."

"We're not paying more than fifteen thousand, no matter what you get us."

I tried not to smile too hard and give away that fifteen is what I had in mind anyway.

It took me two days of off-and-on meetings with Mrs. Goldberg to make headway. Most of the time, I was following her around while she collected rents. She penned a new ten-year lease that included both locations for Jesse and Chris. I got her to include a five-year option with terms to be negotiated in the ninth year of the lease. I also got her to include an option of first refusal if she or her heirs decided to sell the building so that Jesse and Chris would be given the first opportunity to buy the building if an interested party surfaced with an offer.

The brothers gave me a check for fifteen thousand. Jesse told me they already had at least two serious operators interested in leasing the shop.

"I'm not going to say goodbye," I said. "I'll be around."

"You better be," Chris said. He stopped fooling with the meat and looked up at me. "I'm going to miss you."

Jesse and Chris both hugged goodbye, trying hard not to get gore from their bloody aprons on me.

"I'm going to miss you, too," Jesse said. "Come around. Lunch is always on the house."

Years ago, Chris passed away, leaving Jesse with the business. I stayed in touch with Jesse for decades.

I stood in front of the shut-down building. It was still and lifeless, yet much improved from how I had found it. For many years I had passed by this corner, never imagining that I would have a business there, and now that business had come to an end. I remembered everything that had happened there, from the first moment when I drove up and met Ramirez. Now it was gone. It had disappeared as fast as it had begun.

The body shop's new operator had no guarantee they would have those ten cars to paint every day. The volume of business was more than just the location. It was all due to Luis's artistry, Paulo's needles, Susie and Alexa's saucy charm, Mike's sheer muscle, and Elena's incomparable persistence and charisma. It was the synergy of my team and me.

For me, it had been about setting a standard of

excellence, meeting a goal for the customer, and making sure the finished job made them happy.

* * *

It pained me to do it, but I deposited the fifteen thousand to the Whittier Auto Center account at Kitty's bank. I stopped to see her.

"What a surprise," she said. "Are you going to reopen the shop the IRS auctioned off? I heard it went to your friends' next door."

"You miss nothing, Kitty," I said. "No, I was offered the opportunity, but I took a pass. I want another shop, but first, I need to find a location."

"Go back to school, become a professional. With that gift of gab you have, you should go for law."

"I don't think so," I said. "I wish I was smart enough."

"Did you stop just to say hello, or do you need something?"

"You're so direct," I teased. A picture of her naked flashed across my brain.

"Why are you staring?"

"You know Kitty, you really are very beautiful, especially without the glasses."

Her hand went straight to her glasses. She touched them

and almost took them off. "You can be so sweet and such an asshole," she said. I knew she wasn't mad.

"The thirty you loaned me against receivables is paid. I know you know that."

"Yeah, last week Mike brought in the last insurance check, and he wrote a check for the loan interest. I'm going to miss Mike," she said.

"That makes two of us."

I went on after a minute of silence. She was sad about Mike leaving. It showed.

"I need about thirty thousand to clear out from the Whittier Shop. I just put in fifteen that I got for selling my lease on Eastland that I planned to use personally, but that's the way it goes. Anyway, I need fifteen, maybe twenty, not unsecured, same deal. I'll bring you copies of the claims, just like before. When the check comes in the mail, I'll bring it over."

"What's in it for me?"

She had her arms folded across her chest.

"What you want?" I asked.

She looked at me over the top of her glasses. "You are coming to me and not Sam because you want to save the discount; he takes off the top."

"It's not just that. Getting it from you is cleaner. The equipment loan is current, the business account has the fifteen I just put in plus about five thousand, and the credit line you canceled is fully paid."

"I'll do it," she said, "but remember, you owe me."

"I don't need to owe you. Tell me where and when, and I'm there."

She uncrossed her arms, leaned across her desk, and whispered. "You are a marvelous lover."

"It's easy with a woman like you," I said.

My eyes met hers. She stared before she spoke.

"Okay, I'll set something up. Bring me the paperwork tomorrow. It's an easy loan."

"Kitty, thanks. By the way, when I had that furniture company furnish the house I leased for Mike, you mentioned you have a relative in the furniture business."

"I do. My uncle has Garfield Interiors in Montebello."

"I know the place. Didn't know that was your uncle."

"Why do you need furniture?"

"I'm getting married. I plan to lease a house, and I want to do it up really nice."

"Married. I thought you were still married to number three."

"I am, and she's married to number one."

"How will you marry then?"

"Divorce first. Marry after."

"Are you still going to be a bad boy after you get married?"

"Only with you when you want," I lied.

Kitty looked me over like she was a cat and I was a bowl of cream. "When you are ready, I'll fix you up with my uncle. He has it all, including a fabulous decorator that doesn't charge as long as you buy the furniture there."

"Kitty, thanks. I'm going to need your uncle soon.

Chapter 28
Molly Moves In

A few days later, Molly surprised me with an announcement. "I'm moving in," she told me. "We'll make that trip to Guaymas one of these days."

I hugged her. "I love you, sweetheart. We're going to be together now and for as long as we live."

I told Molly about the history of my apartment. Much of it had been witnessed by my tropical fish.

"I have two friends across the way, Ava and Emma. Emma is known to cook up a storm and surprise me when she feels like it, always in the morning. I actually used to live next door to them, across the way from here." Through the window, I pointed out my old apartment.

"I can handle whatever you did before," Molly said, not asking for details. "I will be faithful, and I expect you to be."

It will be difficult," I admitted. "But I love you enough to give it my all. I need to say this, Molly. I didn't cheat ever on my first wife. I didn't cheat ever on my second wife. I didn't cheat on my third wife until we were separated. My bad is I've had sex with a whole bunch of women, but that is not cheating on my vows."

She hugged me and, on my shoulder, said, "You won't need anyone else. I promise."

"I'm so bad," I said.

"We're so bad." She lifted her face, and I saw a smile. "I'm not divorced, and I moved in with you. I'm bad, but this is good bad."

I hugged her. "We have a bumpy ride ahead," I said. "I wish the timing was better."

"The timing is fine as long as we're together. I am looking forward to our mornings together."

"You know I jog in the mornings," I said.

"We will jog in the mornings from now on. Unless you want to do it alone."

That reminded me of Elena, the talker, and how when she first started to jog, she shut up as we started up the steep hill to the top of Monterey Hills and eventually could talk through it.

"I want you to be with me," I said.

Molly parked her yellow car where Elena used to park her

Mustang convertible. The yellow paint would always be a reminder of Elena's mischief.

* * *

When I went looking for a house in Monterey Park, I found a nice corner house with three-bedrooms, three-bathrooms, a den, a spectacular view, and no pool. It was in an up-and-coming neighborhood called the Highlands, not unlike Monterey Hills, where my apartment was located. The rent was two-fifty, unfurnished, but in move-in condition. I was a little anxious when I brought Molly to see it. She was so quiet as we walked through that I didn't know what to think. We stopped in the last room we came to, which was Sylvia's.

"It's beautiful," Molly said, turning a happy face up to me.

"Someday, I'll buy you a huge house," I promised.

"I don't need a huge house." She kissed me. "Just you."

"Soon as I can, I'll buy this house. The owner wants to sell."

"Don't stress. I don't need to own a house. This house is twice as big as the rented house James had for us."

"Just so you know, I paid the rent a year in advance. That way, we can't get thrown out for not paying the rent in case something explodes."

"No one does that," Molly said.

"I've done it before," I said. "I have peace of mind that way."

"You know best," she said, hugging me.

"I love you so much," I said. "I've been looking for you all my life."

I told her about Kitty's uncle's store, Garfield Interiors. She had never met Kitty, and I planned to keep it that way.

"Money is tight," Molly said. "We have a house, and the rent is paid for a year. Why spend a lot of money on furniture and a decorator?"

"I want to do this," I said softly.

She blinked her eyes, looked at me, and nodded.

Kitty had Liz, the decorator, contact me. I gave Liz a key to the house, and she went in to draw a floor plan. When Molly and I visited the store to look at furniture, Liz had possibilities for each room. The third bedroom was intended for a home office. I changed it to quarters for a live-in housekeeper who would take care of Sylvia when needed.

"I've never had a housekeeper before," Molly laughed. "My mom has always taken care of Sylvia. Are you sure you want to spend money on a lady to live in?"

"We'll do it if and when you want to," I said. "The bedroom will be there, just in case."

Molly agreed.

The total cost of the furniture came to eight thousand five hundred dollars. That was so much money then, but you should have seen the furniture. Liz was going to arrange it all for us, even the artwork. Several pieces are still in our home today. Looking back now, the cost of the furniture was a drop in the bucket compared to the money I won in Las Vegas.

Kitty got her uncle to accept $8,000 cash. I paid him from the Vegas winnings that I had in my apartment safe. I loved the feeling that the rent was paid for twelve months and the furniture was fully paid for. Dairy delivery was an option. If there had been a way to figure annual dairy purchases, I would have paid that in advance too. The insecurity of how things can change made me feel vulnerable. We could get slammed.

"Where did you get all that money?" Molly wanted to know.

I told her about my Vegas trip, the last win, about having more wins than losses, and how I didn't plan to go back because it was my turn to lose. I knew it. Mike would say I was crazy to think that way. Maybe I was.

"You can't spend that much money on furniture. Please hon. Don't."

"Too late. It's done. It's for you," I said, taking her in my arms.

"It's too much money," she insisted.

"You and I picked out the furniture, so you know you love it. Stop worrying about it."

The hardest part for me was waiting for the house to be furnished. Some of the pieces were ordered. Liz, the decorator had promised it wouldn't be long.

* * *

After I delivered the last insurance job to the car owner, I let my last body man go. I had given all of them severance pay, though not a lot. I covered Mike's outstanding checks to the two check cashing companies where I continued to flip. Once again, I could have walked away clean.

I still owed taxes for Eastland. I got the credit for the fifteen thousand the sale yielded, but I still owed about fifteen thousand. Sooner or later, they would get me for that. I also owed another eight thousand to the State Board for sales tax. With penalties and interest, the amounts would be crazy high.

When I turned in the keys to the landlord, less than ten thousand dollars in taxes were still owed on the Whittier shop.

"You have a turnkey body shop to rent out," I told him. "The spray booth and oven and compressor are up and running."

"You're a fine young man," he said and stood to shake my hand. "If you ever need a reference, use me."

I swallowed and nodded my appreciation.

"Many thanks for that."

I had no choice but to leave the equipment. It would have cost too much to dismantle the oven and spray booth, and I had no place to store it. I could have taken the compressor, but it would have also been a storage problem. I didn't want to mess with it. I owed Kitty two thousand one hundred dollars on the equipment. I would continue making the payments. The first good money I took in, I'd pay it off.

I stood in front of the huge property before I drove away. Another one bit the dust.

I went through businesses like I went through wives.

I knew Molly would be different.

With no shop to go to, I was ready.

Chapter 29
Guaymas, Mexico

I grabbed Molly and sat her down on the couch, the worn cushions sighing beneath her. She still had that look on her face, a mix of excitement and nerves.

"Honey, let's head for Guaymas," I said, and watched as her expression softened. "We'll get our divorces and get married. There's no reason to wait. I'll feel better if we're married before I meet the rest of your family again."

"Are you sure?" she asked, her voice quiet.

"I'm positive. Aren't you?"

"What about my divorce from James that's still pending here?"

"That can still happen when it happens. Down in Mexico, it's all the same to the court. I've been down this road before, so I know the drill. It's my understanding that it's all legal there because it's legal here." I hated that I had to say that part, but it was the truth.

"I'm game," Molly said, and the nervous knot in my stomach unraveled.

We packed and took Sylvia to stay with her grandmother. It was in the middle of the day. My parents were at work, but I called them on the way out of town. The car smelled like the leather seats and the hint of her perfume.

There were only two hotels in Guaymas, both on the same strip of private beach. As we arrived at the Miramar Hotel, the sun was melting into the water. It painted the sky with streaks of bruised purple and a fiery orange that bled into the calm sea. The hotel was exactly as Pablo had described—isolated and quiet. A little run down, maybe, but that just made it feel more real. The paint on the railings was chipped and faded, and the sliding doors to our bungalow rattled a bit when the breeze picked up. When we got to the front desk, I made arrangements and paid the priest to call and verify with the churches that baptized us to confirm we had been baptized Catholics.

Our bungalow was shaped like a triangle, so every room had a view and direct access to the ocean. We were surrounded by grass on three sides, with sand and ocean in the back. Large sliding glass doors opened right onto the white sand.

I called room service and ordered a feast for four. Molly teased me about my extravagance, but before I'd even finished ordering, she was on my lap, nibbling my ear. We ate a bit of the bread, then decided we were too excited to wait. In the darkness, we ran to the ocean, laughing as we kicked off our shoes and left our clothes in a pile on the sand. The water was unbelievably warm, like a bath left out in the sun all day. We waded in, and I was shocked that even twenty feet out, it was only up to our knees. We knelt down, the soft, silky sand giving way beneath us. The lights from our bungalow and the hotel seemed impossibly far away. All I could hear was the gentle lapping of the water. The moon was a fat, yellow coin hanging so low in the sky it felt like we could reach out and pluck it from the air. Molly settled into my arms. It was just us, the quiet ocean, and the moon. We made our way back, clothes lost somewhere on the sand, wrapped ourselves in towels and dashed to the bungalow, starving, hoping we wouldn't meet anyone on the way.

The dinner I ordered was served on a glass table on the patio just by the sand. We were washed in ocean breezes as we ate. Outdoor candles flickered as we devoured a smorgasbord of dishes: shrimp, oysters, lobster Thermidor, and all the rest of the impressive feast. The food was delicious, but a bit cold by the time we got to it. We went to bed and cuddled one another, sleepy, full of food, and exhausted.

"I love you, forever," I whispered. We sank into a deep and peaceful sleep.

* * *

By seven the next day, we were in the ocean where the water was as warm and calm as the night before. After a hard swim, we relaxed in the water for a while, then jogged along the beach. Molly tackled me, and we rolled on the sand in each other's arms, laughing. To be clear, I was still not a great swimmer then or now, but Molly swam like a pro. I figured if I started to drown or something, she'd save me. I'm not that bad. Remember what I did in boot camp.

By nine thirty, we had met with Pablo's recommended attorney. By noon, we had been granted a divorce in a Mexican court.

As soon as the judge had finished with the divorce proceedings, he stepped off the bench. Still in his black judicial robe, he read us the marriage vows in Spanish. Both Molly and I had tears in our eyes as I put the wedding ring on her finger. She read the inscription inside my ring that said 'Forever.' I had to help her fit the ring on my finger. She was crying too hard to focus on my hand. The judge pronounced us man and wife, and we kissed. The attorney and court clerk acting as witnesses gave us abrazos, embraces. Even the judge got into the act. Memories never to be forgotten.

The next morning, on October 3, 1965, we drove to an old Catholic Church that was getting a facelift. The priest was expecting us and greeted us as we walked to the rectory.

George Hatcher

"I will marry you between masses," the priest said.

We went to the confessional, and while I waited for Molly, I stood in the doorway between the rectory and the church. A few people trickled in for mass, but not many.

Where we were, the only thing not humble was the expansive, infinite ocean. Guaymas was a small fishing city; it had a prodigious fish production, but the town was modest. The church's interior was nice but not a spectacle. The church was airy, with many windows up high, and the altar reached almost to the steeple ceiling. The capacity of worshippers was about a hundred.

When Molly joined me, we followed the priest to the altar and knelt in front of him with our backs to the congregation. Molly looked so lovely that I kept thanking God for giving her to me. Molly was my fourth marriage, but my only marriage in a Catholic church. This marriage was for keeps.

As the priest spoke, I felt my past was swept away and buried. I felt younger than I had in years. I was twenty-three, and Molly was eighteen months older.

When the ceremony was over, Molly and I kissed, then turned around. The church was packed to capacity, and the crowd applauded, totally unplanned. It was amazing. We walked down the aisle to the good wishes of strangers in a wave of smiles and approval as if the world were blessing us.

Two altar boys outside threw rice as we raced for the car. Once inside, Molly fell into my arms.

"Welcome to my family," I whispered to her, breathing in her lovely scent.

"And I welcome you to mine, my love. I welcome you to my heart, my soul, and my body. I'll be good to you for as long as I live."

We kissed.

The car was surrounded by cheering people. Feeling like celebrities loved by the whole world, we waved at them all and drove away.

I'm told that the road to hell is paved with good intentions. My only fear was that she deserved a husband who didn't cheat on her as her ex-husband had done. I was going to give it everything I had to be the man I'd never been able to be in my previous relationships.

Chapter 30
Molly the Beginning

The new house felt like home and was better than any home we'd ever known. We felt as though we were living in a dream. The new furniture looked like it had been designed for the house, and the view of the surrounding suburbs was breathtaking. Liz, the decorator, did a fabulous job of transforming a nice house into a house staged for movie shoots. With the help of a carpentry shop, she added little things: dividers, stand up screens, etc. The house was smaller than the one I had sub-leased to the mortician, but I loved how we fit here.

Molly enrolled Sylvia in kindergarten near the house.

My ex-wife Sophia accepted the copy of the divorce I had gotten in Mexico, but we agreed she would get a local lawyer and file for divorce in Los Angeles. I agreed to pay the costs. She wanted to be sure we were really divorced and that she had legal custody of our daughter Judy.

I learned that Sophia had another man in her life, and it was serious. She would have two children from the new love of her life.

Years after my marriage to Molly, I tried many times to convince Sophia to let Judy live with us, but that was a big no. Judy did visit with us often and became a baby sister to Sylvia.

I won't take you through a step by step of how I acquired the location near Hollywood for my new shop Sunset Auto Center. It took up a little over a hundred lineal feet of Sunset Boulevard with two entrances on the street. The prices in that area were higher than where I'd had my other shops. The tradeoff was that I had to pay higher rent.

The architectural firm that owned the property had been around for ages and had their names on the blueprints of many interesting buildings in California. It would take pages to tell you what I went through to get the owners of that great building to lease it to me and to convert it from a high-end working warehouse to an auto body and paint shop.

George Hatcher

I had to come up with the first and last month's rent and a ten-thousand-dollar deposit.

The president of the firm told me, "If you don't make it, I have to go in and remove the paint equipment and have the roof redone. You want the place; the deposit is $10,000."

This hardball player was also the guy that I leveled with about my other shops closing and the IRS sale. He was an okay person, just too smart not to see the likelihood that I could fail again.

"The only reason we are discussing this possible lease is your transparency about your past failures. You own up to it," he said.

It was good to get a pat on the back like that, but he never wiggled down from his terms that included the big deposit. If Molly had not been in my life, I might have cashed a check somewhere and gone to Vegas in hopes of bringing home a bundle. I remembered all the money I made in Las Vegas and I had nothing to show for it.

I invented the money to get the lease, then I hunted for the money I needed to make it a paint and body shop. It's a terrible way to open a business when you don't have the money, and you float checks like there's money in the bank to cover the paper. I dug a big hole and kept the float going with the support of a check-cashing place that was bigger than any of the places I had dealt with in East Los Angeles. The juice I paid to hold my checks got heavier and heavier as the amount grew. I shared this with no one, not even Molly.

My credit sucked.

I had tax liens from Eastland and the Whittier Shop. I had a credit from the IRS for the sale of the shop at auction, but that didn't pay the full amount I owed. The liens were against the company names; however, the IRS and the State would hold me personally responsible for the amount due. The corporation veil that supposedly protects the owner from personal responsibility has too many loopholes when it comes to tax debt.

The building didn't need sandblasting or painting like my other shops, but I needed equipment, including a spray booth, oven, and compressor. I tried to buy the spray booth, oven, and compressor from the Whittier Shop landlord but learned that he leased the premises to an operator who opened for business a week after finalizing the lease. I had left that shop a turnkey operation.

Chapter 31
The Invitation

Sunset Auto Center was about to open. Molly volunteered to work with me, answering the phones. I hired a live-in maid to take care of Sylvia and do housework. Molly was okay with it because she wanted to be with me. Sylvia was five, in kindergarten. I had a morning routine. I jogged, showered, and left for the shop. I believe the housekeeper walked Sylvia to school and then picked her up the same way. Molly did not jog with me, and that was okay with me.

We trusted the housekeeper, but Molly wasn't used to having a lady living in doing the work and taking care of her daughter.

"Get used to it. We're going to keep her even after you stop working."

She nuzzled my ear.

"Well, okay. I guess I'll need help with all the babies we plan to have."

"I'm thinking eleven more kids. We'll need eleven more nannies."

I thought big about everything. I was twenty-three going on fifteen. Blue Sky.

* * *

My crew was small in comparison to Eastland. They had all worked for me before. I would miss Susie and Alexa, but I planned to work myself. Every day, I thought of Elena, curious about what her plans were, wondering where she was. Florida? Texas? Molly was two handfuls, so I didn't miss Elena for sex. I missed Elena because she was my friend.

I banked with Kitty, but I didn't travel twenty miles from Sunset to her branch. A branch was six blocks from the shop. I did talk to her often.

"Remember, you owe me," she always said.

Molly and I stood outside the shop and liked what we saw. Bright banners and colorful signs advertised, 'We paint your car while you wait for $45. *Bodywork, tiny or huge.*' Just a few minutes from Hollywood, the traffic on Sunset Boulevard was twice the traffic count I had at the main shop that had been the cash cow. I believed I had to do as much or more business on Sunset.

The Sunset shop didn't take off as fast as Eastland had. The forty-five dollar paint job attracted people who inquired. If the person decided to paint the car, the one-day turnover wasn't the hook. I had to sell each job, so it was me. Most of the time, the customer opted out of the forty-five dollar job and jumped to a seventy-five or hundred dollar paint job. I preferred doing the lower-priced job because it was quicker, and I trusted the paint we used. It was reliable, beautiful, and the same as I had used at Eastland.

A whole mess of car dealers were in Hollywood, and I got out there to pass out business cards and talk to the used car bosses. That left my painter, Luis, to cover new customers while I was away. I did not have a Mike or Elena to sell when I wasn't there or when I was there and busy.

My first stop was a Ford dealership a few blocks away. I gave the used car manager a foldout brochure with a picture of the shop, a color chart, a price list, and my pitch.

"Eric Hughes charges twenty-nine ninety-nine. Why would I want to pay forty-five?"

"My paint doesn't peel. And if you don't like it, pay fifteen, and I'll paint it again."

"That's the guarantee?"

"Yes, the customer pays fifteen dollars if something goes wrong, if it fades in the first two years, or if he hates the color when he picks up the car."

"Interesting," he said, thoughtfully. He smiled. "I'll call you to come get a couple of cars on Monday."

* * *

I went to a Dodge agency and charmed the owner's daughter, an attractive young woman named Julie, who was second in command. I took her for a two-margarita lunch and promised her a fee if she referred other agencies to me.

"If I like the work you do, you can use me as a reference. I want ten dollars cash for every car I send you."

"Julie, I'm getting forty-five dollars. How can I give you a ten and pickup and deliver?"

"I'll send the cars and pick them up. Most of the jobs will have some bodywork. You'll do okay, I promise."

I gave her a look, then smiled.

"You have a deal." I reached into my pocket and pulled out a $20 dollar bill. "There's more where that came from."

Her smile was as happy as Donna's when I gave her two hundred for the night.

"I need to supplement my income. My father is cheap," she explained.

We had lunch again a few days later when I saw she was as good as her word on sending jobs my way. Back at Sunset,

I apologized to Molly for missing another lunch with her. At Sunset, everyone lunched at the same time, noon to one. If a customer came in, I handled. If I wasn't there, then the person in charge handled it. I wondered what Elena would have thought of everyone having lunch at the same time.

Molly hushed me with a kiss.

"I understand. Besides, lunch here with the crew is a riot. I laugh so much that I barely eat. I'm learning how to mask cars."

"I love you," I said, feeling like the luckiest man alive. "You don't need to mask; you will lose your nails."

"I will not. I like to mask."

To cover the windshield with paper and tape it to the weatherstrip, Molly had to use a ladder. I watched her from afar. Soon she kept a blade between her teeth in easy reach. She was good.

Elena had never masked, and neither had Susie and Alexa, but they were good at selling and getting the cars out that were promised at a given hour. Molly didn't want to learn how to sell and insisted that masking was no big deal to her.

Did Molly and I have quickies during working hours? You bet we did. The office was much larger than the one at Eastland, plus it was not built over a walk-in refrigerator and freezer. I never had to worry about the floor collapsing if the sex became intense.

George Hatcher

* * *

Business was steady, but not even close to ten cars a day. However, the average price per car was double what it was at Eastland. Car dealers sent me business, and they preferred paying at the end of the month. The good thing is that it wasn't like trying to collect from insurance companies. Those in charge were understanding. A couple of days after doing the job, I picked up a check. Julie at the Dodge dealership wanted an extra five, promising to deliver a check when she sent for the cars. I gave her the extra five. She was right that the cars she sent were more than the base paint price of forty-five dollars. The average ticket price was seventy-five dollars.

* * *

The check cashing company I was doing business with was owned by a guy who reminded me of Sam but not a nice fatherly Sam. He was a roughneck. I don't recall for sure, but I think he was Armenian, at least three decades older than me.

"As long as you keep paying me the juice once a week, I'll keep holding the check or checks." That was the deal. I went from him trusting me with ten thousand dollars to three times that much by the time I opened the Sunset shop. The fee was the juice. He never let me forget that, at some point, he needed to deposit the checks.

"This paper is growing whiskers," he said, referring to the checks he was holding.

"I'll bring you new ones and take the cash you give me to cover the ones with whiskers, easy."

He played it like this was new. Occasionally, I gave him a new set of checks for about the same amount he was holding. He gave me the cash, and I took to the bank to deposit the money. It was the same thing I had done with Chester and the others. The difference was that Hank was savvier and charged more interest. I didn't have to do the cash exchange as fast as in the past.

The shop made enough money to pay the help, rent, and everything that it took to run the business. Since I didn't have good credit, everything was paid with cash, except the paint and paint supplies. The vendor wanted my business badly, and he knew I had a big investment in the spray booth, oven, compressor, and other equipment. Once my bill hit five hundred, he came over, and I'd pay him off and start all over. Five hundred was a lot of money then. Minimum wage was a dollar twenty-five an hour. The ten spot I gave Julie for each car plus another five on delivery was a lot of money, too.

Good credit is always important, but the Chevrolet dealer who was sending me business fixed it so that I got a brand-new Corvette for less than five hundred down. I recall paying less than four thousand for the sports car. I gave Molly my cherry Impala. She gave her yellow car to a relative.

I called Donald, my CPA. He came to check out the layout.

"I can come out once a month, and I'll get you a payroll service to do your payroll checks every two weeks."

"Don, later for the payroll. I still have payroll taxes I owe for Eastland. I'm paying everyone cash. I don't want to mess up the sales tax. I need it figured out, and I will pay it for sure."

Don agreed. I wasn't a block away any longer, but I wasn't in Timbuktu. The drive wasn't that far. From his office, he didn't even need to take the freeway.

"You need to get insurance," Don told me. "You know the drill."

"I have car insurance for the cars. I can't handle everything right now."

Don shook his head. "I will keep bugging you," he promised.

"That's okay. Eventually, I will do it all by the book."

* * *

I hired a full-time girl, Martina. She was the plainest girl on the face of the earth, twenty-five, a mild-looking blonde with blue eyes, no curves at all and no make-up, but smart. She would have made a perfect model in today's world.

She couldn't possibly remind me of Elena, but she did. Every time I looked at Martina, my memory of Elena superimposed itself. I adored Molly, but I missed Elena's presence. Molly was thrilled with Martina. I knew why.

Molly stopped coming to work with me and stayed home. She didn't say so, but I knew that's what she really wanted to do. She had free time to see her brothers and sisters and friends that she didn't get to see much working with me. I missed her for the first few days, but I was happy she was keeping busy at home and able to socialize.

* * *

I called Kitty.

"I know you have something up your sleeve to suddenly ask me to lunch," she said.

I took her to a steak house on Olympic Boulevard in Montebello, where there was no entertainment.

"I owe a check cashing place thirty-two thousand dollars, and the weekly juice I am paying him is killing me."

"Why don't you ask Sam?"

"My shop is too far for him to deliver parts. I prefer not to bother him. I've owed you a lot more than thirty-two thousand in the past, and I paid it back."

"George, I have to run a credit check for the file, and I don't think it's going to be very good. How did you get that Corvette?"

I sidetracked the reply. "I do car dealer work. The manager got me approved. I feel good owning the car, and I gave my car to my wife."

"How's your marriage?"

We started to eat.

"We're happy. All good. She was working with me, but I asked her to stay home."

"How will you pay back the loan if I can swing it?"

"You tell me."

"Can you do a thousand a month?"

"I can do five hundred, and I promise I'll get it paid off sooner rather than later."

After we finished eating but before we got up to leave, she asked, "What's in it for me?"

In a low voice, I said, "I will fuck you for two hours straight."

A week later, I paid off the check cashing joint.

"Hank, I totally appreciate how you helped me and especially the trust you have placed in me for so long."

He smiled. "Kid, don't say goodbye. I know you will be back."

I nodded. "I never say never."

We shook hands, and I went back to the shop. I had been paying him three hundred a week. It was like burning money.

* * *

At a small party I gave at home, Judge Black warned me, "If I hear of you giving away any free paint jobs or other work, I'll jail you. And that includes any work you do for me or Luca."

"Better listen, kid," Luca threatened. "Or else!"

My friends believed my past failures stemmed from offering 'freebies,' but that wasn't the real issue. Fast-forward: I found myself owning a downtown Los Angeles Mexican restaurant. While I did offer freebies to judges, politicians, and other influential figures, I'm convinced that this was not the reason the company ultimately went bankrupt. The truth is, I'm just a terrible administrator. My poor management skills, lack of strategic planning, and inability to effectively oversee operations were the real culprits behind the downfall of the business.

* * *

Molly had five sisters and three brothers, and each sibling had kids, a bunch. It was not uncommon for Molly's brothers and sisters to come over for drinks and food on a Saturday, and on Sunday morning, the living room, dining room, and sometimes even a hallway or two would be packed with the sleepovers. In the morning, the ladies would congregate in the kitchen and prepare breakfast for everyone. I had never experienced such a close relationship with family before. Sophia had a big family, but it wasn't like Molly's.

I enjoyed their company and looked forward to the sleepovers. We listened to music and drank, or we'd play poker, sometimes with two tables going. I dug it. Molly's brothers and sisters were like a clique. They were best friends like they couldn't get tired of each other.

Here we are, decades later. Molly has two living sisters and one brother. Molly's two sisters hunkered down for months during the pandemic of 2020 living with us. It is a blessing that they are together, happy to be keeping each other company.

* * *

The problem.

I started drinking Canadian Club again. No one in the group went for wine, so it was either beer or CC for me. Beer would put on the pounds in no time. I suppose that hard liquor can do the same. My weight yo-yoed up and down. My best fitness was when I jogged hard. I would get burned out on jogging and miss it for weeks, sometimes months. Molly liked to drink, and she smoked one cigarette after dinner. I probably drank five drinks to her one. I never drank during the day but made up for it after hours. I didn't smoke. Years later, I would start smoking cigars.

* * *

I received a surprise phone call from my former employee Susie.

"How did you find me?" I asked her.

I missed that little laugh of hers, sexy, mysterious.

"It was easy. Listen, I want to talk to you about something."

The Susie who met me for lunch was not the girl I remembered.

"You look great!"

"So, do you, Chief."

She was wearing a dress and high heels and had a new, feathery hairstyle. She was a knock-out. What am I saying? She was always a knock-out, but she did look different.

"Guess where I'm working?"

"Not at Eric Hughes again?"

"Guess again."

"You tell me."

"I'm an insurance adjuster for Golden West!"

"You gotta be joshing me!"

Shaking her head, she grinned. "Nope. Serious."

She handed me her business card.

The last thing I wanted was to get mired in insurance work again, but Susie's proposal was too good to turn down. I listened with growing excitement.

Susie was a field adjuster. Her job was to inspect wrecked vehicles for people her company insured. If the repair estimate she wrote was under a thousand dollars, her company allowed her to write a draft payable to both the insured and the body shop of choice. When the job was completed, the insured endorsed the check, and I would do the same and bank it. It was almost the same as the work I used to do for Farmers Insurance once upon a time, except that Farmers didn't have a thousand-dollar limit.

"What's in it for Susie?" I asked.

She licked her lips. "You tell me," she said. "A fuck now and then. And some much-needed cash."

I stared at her pretty face. All the memories came flooding back: Susie and me, Elena and Susie and me, Elena, Alexa, and Susie and me—steaming memories.

"I remember when all you had to do was unbutton your jeans and let them drop."

"I can get out of these clothes just as fast. Tell me where and when."

"The problem is that you're addictive."

I stared at her face longer than necessary.

"Your loss, Jefe," she said with a grin. "How about five percent of the invoice?"

"You got it," I said.

I kissed her. The kiss went on way too long.

When our lips were no longer attached but still close. "I still have the scent of you in my nostrils," I said. "I don't mean your fragrance right now, either."

"Jefe, you are such a turn-on. Why did you get married again?"

"I love her. Molly is for keeps."

"She's lucky."

"No, she's not," I said. "I'm the lucky one."

"Don't be so hard on yourself," Susie said. She kissed the tip of my nose and started for the door. "Get ready for some business."

"You made my day," I said. She was walking away. "Have you heard from Elena?" I asked. She stopped and turned to face me.

"She calls, always at night. She's in Hawaii with him. She got excited when I told her about this job."

"I thought she hated Hawaii. She said it was boring."

"Should I tell her anything from you?"

"Yeah. Tell her I want only the best for her."

"I'll tell her."

* * *

During the drive home, I thought of Elena in Hawaii. In the wine room, she had said that she drank way too much out of boredom. She probably drives around in a Rolls Royce now. Before Eastland got shut down, I had Susie deliver her car from my apartment to her aunt's house, a tiny gift for all she did for me.

All in all, my day was productive. I was in terrific spirits when I hugged and kissed Molly and Sylvia, who were waiting for me at the door. The scent of Molly's My Sin perfume mixed with the faint aroma of Sylvia's freshly baked cookies filled the air, instantly lifting my mood.

When I arrived home, the mental replays of Elena and Susie stopped. Molly was that powerful. Her presence was like a warm blanket, wrapping me in comfort and security.

That night, as we lay in bed with the lights out, the room was filled with the soft hum of the ceiling fan. "Remember Susie, who worked with me at the main shop?" I asked, my voice barely above a whisper.

Molly's face rested on my chest, her hair inches from my mouth, smelling faintly of coconut shampoo. "I remember her. She worked with Elena and the other girl writing invoices," she replied, her breath warm against my skin.

I kissed the top of her head, feeling the softness of her hair against my lips. "You have a good memory."

"How can I not have a good memory about her and the other two when you told me how you'd roll around in bed with them at your apartment," she said, her tone tinged with a mix of sarcasm and hurt. "At the same time," she added.

"Hon, don't be like that," I pleaded, wondering why I had brought it up, though I knew I had to tell her Susie was going to be around.

"You brought her up for a reason. Tell me," she insisted, her voice firm yet gentle.

I took a deep breath and told Molly about Susie being an insurance adjuster and the talk we'd had over lunch about her sending business our way.

"Sounds like she's back in," Molly said, her voice laced with suspicion.

"She's not back in like you think," I assured her.

Molly pulled away from my chest, her face directly above mine. When she spoke, I could smell the minty freshness of Pepsodent Toothpaste on her breath. "Keep it business, Hon."

I kissed her softly. "For sure. It's just business," I promised, hoping to ease her worries.

Molly learned that when James was released from jail, he moved in with Adrian. I wondered if she was happy. I hoped she was. I also hoped that James would not give us problems with a recently approved visitation agreement for him to see Sylvia. If I happened to be home and answered the phone when he was calling for Sylvia, he always had attitude.

"Let me talk to my daughter, punk," he spat. Anger surged through me, but I forced myself to stay calm. If he dared to say that to my face, he wouldn't find me so composed.

Susie's referrals came in. Gradually the pace increased. The work I got from street traffic, referrals from those clients who left satisfied, used car dealers, and Susie's clients, we banged away twelve hours a day. Profit reflected growth. Growth meant I could no longer pull my painter or bodyman to sell if I was not on the floor. Susie got Alexa to call me.

"Jefe, Susie says you need help."

"Hey stranger, I miss you," I said.

"Not nearly as much as I miss you," she said.

Alexa quit her job at another body shop. Within a week, she came to work for me.

That night, I told Molly about hiring Alexa. Molly knew I needed help and was actively looking for someone.

"Little by little, you will have everyone like you had before."

"Hon, I had a great crew there. Alexa can sell. She knows the business really well."

"Keep it business Hon," she said calmly. "I trust you."

We didn't get the morning rushes like we used to. There were no more rushes of ten people dropping off their cars for paint jobs within two hours of opening, but we were busy. With Alexa there, I was free to visit the car dealers more often. I'd take bottles of booze and other small gifts to the ones sending me business. Julie at Dodge, whose payback was fifteen dollars per car, I'd take her to lunch frequently. We took to each other.

"You're the only dude ever that never makes a pass at me." She was on her second margarita. Julie was staring at me. "I dig your hair and eyes." I thought about the women in my life who had messed with my hair. Elena was on my mind.

My eyes met her. I was sitting across from her at a local bar and grille restaurant not far from the shop. "Julie, you are the hottest woman I have ever met."

Julie laughed. "Now that's a bunch of bull."

Molly came by work. We planned to go out for lunch together. Before we left the shop she stopped and said hello to Alexa. She gave Susie a friendly kiss on the cheek.

"She quit a job to come help me," I said. "She's a dynamite salesperson." Molly already knew this.

"I'm happy you are here to help him," Molly told Alexa.

At lunch, Molly said, "Alexa is very pretty. Have you noticed?"

"You know I noticed," I said. "That doesn't mean I touch."

Molly smiled from across the table. "Was she one of the girls that slept with Elena and you?"

"Hon, you already know the answer. You know that the girl sending me the insurance business was part of it as well."

Molly sighed and put down her fork. "I've asked you before," she said. "Why?"

"By why, you mean why three women in bed?"

"You know what I mean."

"It's the past," I said. "Let's not go there again."

I extended my hand. She put her fork down and rested her hand on mine.

"I love you," I said.

"I know you do. Change of subject?" she offered, smiling brightly.

"I'm having the fried ice cream," I said.

"We are having fried ice cream," she said with that smile that made me feel good.

* * *

When I accumulated a little cushion at the bank, I started talking about finding another shop.

"It's your call," Molly said. "But tell me tomorrow when you're sober."

"Hon, I'm sober."

Grinning, she shook her head. "You will be in the morning."

"Hon, I'm sober," I insisted.

Molly knew how to handle every situation. I knew she didn't want me to open another shop. She'd heard the stories of the shops I opened then had to shut down. She'd heard the stories of all that money I won in Las Vegas and how I had nothing to show for it.

Of all my confessions, I believe what troubled her the most was the locker thing.

"Disgusting," she said to me more than once. "You were on parole. You could have been sent back."

But no matter what I told Molly, I knew she loved me, and she knew I loved her.

* * *

Donald, my accountant, went a little crazy when he heard about another shop.

"What you should do," Donald said, "is find your promissory notes from Eastland and make deals. You can buy them back for ten cents on the dollar. Scratch that, pay the IRS and state. That's more important for now. Then pay the promissory notes. If you have cash left over, buy a house for you and Molly. You have everything you need in this shop. Keep in mind you can't be in two places at once, and you're the man who makes everything work."

"I think you're getting grumpy," I joked.

"I want to see you make it all the way this time," he said.

I knew he was right. I ignored the advice about paying off the debts I left behind but stopped talking about another shop because I didn't have a spot in mind. I had no sex going on the side, and the least I could do is dream about what's next, business-wise. I had no plans to settle for one shop. With the insurance work and getting paid right after finishing the job, I was making money. I had real cash flow without having to cash checks.

The tradeoff—and there's always a tradeoff when there's something good going on—I had a great deal with the insurance work Susie was sending me, but I had to hire more help. I couldn't continue to pay everyone cash, especially after a painter's helper's right foot was run over by a car being moved in the shop.

Donald set up a payroll service. I had to buy workers' compensation insurance. I broke down and got liability insurance for the business that I had been operating without for more than a year. It was like déjà vu.

I accepted an invitation from my bail bondsman friend, Luca Valle. I told Molly about it—a party in Mexico City. We'd have one day to explore the city. A couple of days before the event, Luca called.

"Can't make it, kid. I'm sick. Can't travel right now.

"We won't go either," I said quickly.

"Pablo will be disappointed."

"I'd feel out of place going alone, Luca. I'm not in that league. I like Pablo, but he won't even know I'm not there. Let me pass. You know I like him, but—"

"He likes you too. He's looking down the road for when Mexican business people here will contribute to campaigns there. Pablo sees you as an organizer, like I've been for many others. You know how I come around for donations. They need me and others like me."

"It's going to be tremendously embarrassing when he learns I lost my shops, and what if he digs and finds out I was in prison once?"

Luca laughed, but it was really a growl like the Judge did from time to time. "You were never in prison, kid. It was juvenile hall. I've told you that before."

"Juvenile Hall, my ass. DVI is prison."

Now Luca laughed. "Kid, please go with Molly to Mexico City."

I went silent, letting him convince me.

Luca continued. "It's good he needs something from you. He's on his way to the top. From a small-time mayor of Tijuana to the capitol as governor. From there to president. This party is not to help him become governor. That's a done deal. His backers are paving the road for him to become president someday. You'll meet powerful people there. With your gift of gab, they will love you. It's an entrée. You've got to go."

"I can't afford any big donations right now," I said.

"Later, you do what I do. Go around and get others to donate. You don't need that on this trip. Kid, go."

"Okay, I'll go. I want to know one thing. What makes you so interested in politics down south?"

"I have interests down there. It's important to me who's governor of Baja and who's president of the country."

"I thought you were just a bail bondsman." It was a lame thing for me to say.

He laughed.

"I have stuff going in many places, kid. I'm sort of like you that way. Fingers in more than one pie. I'm crazy."

"You are not crazy," I said.

He coughed. "Kid, I'm getting over the hill. If it came down to it, I don't need Pablo or anyone else. For that matter they need me and my contributions. You, you're a different story. A young man just starting out. You'll pay your dues here and there, and someday you can rake in a bag full of favors. There are millions to be made in Mexico. Consider Pablo more than a friend. Consider him an investment."

Chapter 32
A World Apart

When the invitation came from Pablo's friend, Rodolfo, we didn't know quite what to expect. We packed our bags for Mexico City, unaware that the trip would drop us into a world far removed from our own.

Rodolfo sent a car to meet us at the airport and drive us to the María Isabel Hotel. To my surprise, it turned out to be a limousine. It felt out of place — no doubt meant for Luca, not for Molly and me.

"A taxi would've been fine," I muttered.

Molly laughed. "Don't worry about it. Let's just enjoy the ride."

The hotel hadn't changed much since I'd last seen it. Still elegant, still proud of its history. Molly admired the room while I struggled with my formal jacket in the mirror. I wasn't used to looking so polished, and the reflection staring back didn't feel like the man I knew. Molly, on the other hand, looked radiant. She twirled in her gown, lighthearted and confident, while I fussed with my tie.

When the driver returned, we were taken to Rodolfo's house — or rather, his mansion. From the outside it looked more like a palace. Cars lined the driveway, valets darted back and forth, and guests ascended wide marble steps. I felt like Cinderella in borrowed clothes, waiting for midnight to reveal the real me: a paint-and-body man from Los Angeles.

Inside, the scene was no less intimidating. The crowd was elegant, the atmosphere charged. Pablo spotted us quickly and greeted us warmly, which eased my nerves. He introduced us to ministers, corporate heads, and officials from Pemex. I smiled, nodded, and worked my Spanish as best I could, while Molly charmed everyone she met with her natural warmth.

By the time we returned to the hotel, I was drained. "They made me out to be someone I'm not," I admitted.

"Don't be so hard on yourself," Molly said. "Everyone was kind."

But lying awake that night, my thoughts wouldn't rest. The evening had been dazzling, but it left me uneasy. I felt the urgency to grow, to build more shops, to invest, to get ahead. The world I had stepped into that night was far from my own — and yet, part of me wanted to reach for it.

Chapter 33
Back To Reality

That restless night in Mexico City stayed with me long after we returned home. Back in Los Angeles, I threw myself into the shops with renewed urgency. It wasn't enough just to keep things running — I felt driven to expand, to open more locations, to build something that would prove I belonged in bigger rooms. Every late-night thought circled the same point: how far could I push it before something gave way?

Two days later, when I was back at real work in the real world, I got a call from Susie. It pulled me off the floor but I didn't take it in my office. I turned over the walk-in potential customer over to Alexa. She gave me a thumbs up, and I grabbed the phone extension close to the front door.

"Did you have fun in Mexico?"

"Believe it," I yelled back over the sound of the grinder. The phone had a long line attached to it that actually reached outside. I stepped out, leaning against the facade, leaving machine noises inside. Traffic was quiet, at least in comparison to bodywork.

"Then why did you come back so soon?"

"I don't have the luxury of taking a vacation yet." A woman pulled up in the lot dropping a man off. I changed which wall I was leaning on so he didn't tangle in the phone cord, and he nodded his head at me as he walked in. I recognized him as the cherry red Impala, a five hundred fifty dollar job. One of Susies.'

"You're really going to want to celebrate when I tell you what I've done."

"I'm listening," I said.

"My supervisor has agreed. He's given me green lights! Doesn't matter if you open another shop or if you keep the one shop. I have a GO!

"Go what? What are you talking about?"

"I can send jobs to you officially. No more under-cover work. You are now a one stop shop for us."

"Joshing me?"

"And you haven't heard it all. I've got my boss around my little finger, as well as other parts of my anatomy. I can now write a draft on the spot, as always, but listen to this: no more thousand-dollar limit!"

My heart jumped. I held the phone away from my face for an instant and said to no one in particular, and the traffic in general, "Yes!" and punched the air over my head. I could hear Susie talking, and put the phone back to my ear.

"Let me finish. There's a catch."

"I'd be suspicious if there weren't."

"I get ten percent instead of five, 'cause I got to split it with my boss-man. Means I get less, but it's okay."

"If you can do the volume, you'll make more," I said.

"I plan to, but I need the claims to be at least close to your shop. You know the drill. Not as easy as it seems."

"I know the drill, and I love the good news, and I have no problem with the catch. How about loan cars?"

"No loaners required. If our customer has coverage for rental, we pay for rental. If not, they on their own."

"Lovely," I said. "I really gotta thank you for this."

"You can do that any time." She made a big show of sighing on the phone. "Too bad you got married again."

"You keep saying that. Besides, you have your boss wrapped around your anatomy." I chuckled. It didn't bother me. This was how Susie was. She kept drilling away.

"You're so mean, Jefe. He ain't nothing like you."

"That is probably a good thing," I said.

* * *

Susie was sending me two or three jobs a week. The average was five hundred a car, and I got paid right away. With this new deal, if the average was a thousand, I'd be delighted, but the bigger the wreck, the longer it takes to do, the more parts to front. I was happy that she could freely send the business. As long as they paid fast, it didn't matter if the jobs stayed in the range they were. Was I excited about the new deal? Yes.

Don was always on me.

"Be smart son. Don't spoil what you got by opening another place. It's risky. You know it is."

I laughed. "At the moment, there can't be another shop anyway. All this talk about opening number two and I haven't the faintest idea where it would be."

Don grinned wide enough that I saw his gums and tonsils.

"That is music to my ears," he said.

* * *

Even though I was getting paid on delivery for anything Susie sent me, I needed to front the money for parts and materials. I needed more labor. I went back to Hank, the check casher. We met in his office closeted like Fort Knox behind the steel door and bullet-proof glass. He had a commercial coffee pot going. I poured myself a cup, bitter but at least it was hot.

"You got to give me a better deal on the juice," I said.

"I have overhead like you. When I give you money, I lose the use of that money to cash checks. Look at the line out there waiting."

The juice had been cheaper with Chester and the others. I was stuck with Hank and his bigger charges. I left behind three check cashers whose promissory notes for the bounced checks I never covered. Once I made it big, I'd go back and clean up the mess I left behind. I swallowed the dregs of the coffee, dumped the foam cup in his trash, and left with a bitter taste in my mouth.

I still had no rent to pay but the year was almost up. I was sorely tempted to cash a check and fly up to Vegas. I knew if I scored, I could buy the house without a bank involved. But superstition rode my back. I was due to lose. I couldn't afford to come back a loser. Before, it was just me. Now, I had to consider Molly.

At the shop, I watched every job as if it was my own car. Small job, big job, it didn't matter. Every vehicle out the door had to be perfect. With Alexa there to sell, I had time. It was getting to be busy.

I should mention that Martina, Alexa, and I were now doing the selling. This particular morning, we had a walk-in.

Martina rushed to greet him, and as she passed me, turned to look in my direction and bumped into the empty trash bin. She turned a bright red, righted the empty bin, and looked at me as if she was checking to see if I noticed. I pointed to the customer. She turned a brighter red and continued on. I put my hand to my chin, rubbing it.

"You look thoughtful, Jefe," Alexa said. She was sitting alone at a table we use with customers, and checking over some paperwork. "Peso for your thoughts?"

I had noticed Martina stared at me a lot.

"Did you tell Martina about my apartment days?" I asked Alexa.

She looked up from the papers, eyebrows high, looking surprised.

"Jefe, why do you ask that?"

"She stares at me a lot," I said.

"Jefe, she's only fantasizing."

"Stop with the nonsense."

"Maybe she has a crush on you, Jefe."

"Alexa, all that stuff was secret."

"I promise not to mention anything again." She crossed her hand over her heart.

I let it pass because I liked her, and we had history. I felt that if Molly had been working at the shop as before, even though I had told her about my apartment days, had she heard rumors or gossip started by an employee about me, she would have exploded.

I had not forgotten that Adrian told me Molly cornered her about her husband James. Molly had slapped her hard. When Adrian slapped her back, Molly punched her and knocked the wind out of her.

I cashed small checks with Hank. As soon as I had the extra cash on deposit, I would call him and tell him how much to deposit.

"I can cover one of the five thousand. Go ahead and deposit."

"Will do, Kid."

"Hank, be sure to cut the juice on that five today."

"Will do, Kid. Anything else?"

"Yes, have a good rest of the day, my friend."

Chapter 34
Been Here Done This Before

It was Friday morning, and I was working the floor with Alexa. We each had a customer. Mine was looking at color samples, wanting to paint her car. Alexa was deeper in the process with a guy and his truck. I heard a car door slam, a sound that cut through the low thrum of the shop, and looked toward one of the entrances. A black sedan came to a stop. Another car pulled up, blocking the other entrance.

Alexa was twenty feet away, but she saw what I saw. Our eyes met across the shop floor. I read her lips.

"Cops."

I took a few steps toward the parking lot. Four men stepped out of one car, two from the other. All of them walked in. The tallest one flashed a badge. They weren't cops. IRS.

He was a bald man with a chin so square it looked chiseled from granite. His face was all harsh lines, his cheeks hollowed out like he hadn't eaten in a month. I couldn't see any eyebrows above his pale eyes, which made his stare feel flat and soulless. The air around him felt heavy, like a storm front rolling in. My stomach twisted into a knot. The scent of paint fumes, a smell I'd worked with for years, now made me want to gag. My heart hammered against my ribs like it was trying to punch its way out. The IRS had caught up with me. They had a demand for money I owed from way back. I didn't have it.

The customers were allowed to leave with their cars. All employees—including me—were given fifteen minutes to leave. We could take nothing but our personal property. I voluntarily turned over the keys. Martina made a quick list of the owners of each car being worked on.

The agent in charge said an agent would be back to let the owners pick up their cars the next day at ten. They were only interested in cash and assets that could be sold at public auction. Any unclaimed car would be impounded and towed.

At least Molly wasn't here to see this. I started gathering what I could and told Martina, "Have everyone follow you to Margarito's. I'll meet you there, and we can pay everyone."

"Are you sure?" Martina asked, her voice tight.

I forced a smile, the kind that didn't reach my eyes. As a good husband this time around, I'd been determined to ignore all women, not my wife. I met Martina's eyes for the first time in weeks, and in them, I saw a flash of fear I hadn't put there.

"He's sure," Alexa said, stepping between us, her voice calm as a knife in a sheath. "We'll be there, Jefe."

Half an hour after the IRS had arrived, Sunset Auto Center was padlocked from the outside. IRS warning signs blanketed every exterior surface.

I drove over to Hank's. He didn't know what had just happened. He was holding seven thousand in checks. I knew it would be easy to get five thousand, more than enough to make a final payroll.

"Hank, I need half of it in small, twenties, tens, fives, and twenty-five in singles."

"You got it, kid."

I had no idea how I would pay Hank back. For the present, he would have to wait. I had thirteen workers who needed a little severance and their final pay.

I went on to the restaurant. For nine of my workers, this wasn't new. They'd been through the same drill back at Eastland. But it was still totally unexpected and devastating to all of us.

I drove home to Molly and Sylvia.

About the Author

George Hatcher is a man who has always believed that the world is full of opportunities waiting for those bold enough to seize them. With a ninth-grade education and a wealth of unique experiences, he has faced the ups and downs of life head-on. At the age of 20, while serving time, George took the initiative to complete the assignments and tests necessary to earn his high school diploma. His own life is a treasure trove of stories waiting to be uncovered.

Over the years, George has enjoyed a diverse career as an entrepreneur, consultant, and strategist. He has served as a peacemaker for athletes and their parents, as well as a crisis management advisor for physicians and attorneys, achieving considerable success in client development and public relations. He is a licensed boxing manager in California, though he currently has no boxers signed.

George has logged over 200,000 air miles annually through business travel and pleasure trips with his wife. However, since the onset of COVID-19 in 2020, his travel has come to a halt. Now, in retirement, George finds that life remains an ongoing adventure. Unfortunately, he is fighting several new battles that he never anticipated, yet he continues to discover something new with each step.

As a passionate storyteller, George has published over twenty books and finds immense joy in writing. With the world opening up again, he has seized the opportunity to immerse himself fully in his literary pursuits. He currently resides in Rancho Mirage, California, with his wife, Molly, his partner for 60 years, and their home is filled with three cats and one macaw named Peaches. Each experience in his life has taught him invaluable lessons about adaptability, perseverance, and a touch of luck. Like the person who hits their head just to feel the pleasure of stopping, George has made his share of mistakes—some more than once. He hopes others can learn from them as he has.

Now devoted entirely to writing, George Hatcher invites others to join him on this remarkable journey, filled with lessons and stories that showcase the beauty of life's unpredictability.

A longer bio is on his website at http://georgehatcher.com/bio/bio.html

www.ingramcontent.com/pod-product-compliance
Lightning Source LLC
Chambersburg PA
CBHW071403130526
44581CB00016B/149/J